Advance Praise for
From Wall Street to the White House and Back

"I talked about embracing failure in my book, and I can say that Anthony's book is a great tool for anyone that wants to learn how to bounce back from setbacks and failure."
—Arnold Schwarzenegger, 38th Governor of the State of California

"Love him or hate him, there is nobody quite like my friend 'The Mooch.' From the world of finance to DC, his illustrious career is filled with successes, failures, and most importantly, stories, that only Anthony could tell. His experience both leading up to, and following, his eleven memorable days in the Trump White House is the kind of unique journey that makes this book a real page-turner, filled equally with lessons, laughs, and an in-depth look into the life of one of the most interesting people I know."
—Robert Wolf, Founder of 32 Advisors and former Chairman of UBS Americas

"We all fall. We all know life will bring struggle and suffering. The idea that 'what doesn't kill you makes you stronger' is only true if you know how to turn a challenge into an opportunity. That's what Anthony teaches us in this book. It is a gift."
—Chris Cuomo, Anchor at NewsNation

Also by Anthony Scaramucci

*The Sweet Life with Bitcoin: How I Stopped Worrying
about Cryptocurrency and You Should Too!*

The Genius of Algorand: Technical Elegance and the DeFi Revolution

*Goodbye Gordon Gekko: How to Find Your
Fortune Without Losing Your Soul*

*The Little Book of Hedge Funds: What You Need to Know
About Hedge Funds But the Managers Won't Tell You*

Hopping Over the Rabbit Hole

From
WALL STREET
to the
WHITE HOUSE
and BACK

The Scaramucci Guide to
UNBREAKABLE RESILIENCE

ANTHONY SCARAMUCCI

Published by SALT BOOKS
An Imprint of POST HILL PRESS
ISBN: 978-1-63758-463-7
ISBN (eBook): 978-1-63758-464-4

From Wall Street to the White House and Back:
The Scaramucci Guide to Unbreakable Resilience
© 2024 by Anthony Scaramucci
All Rights Reserved

Cover design by Conroy Accord

Post Hill Press
New York • Nashville
posthillpress.com

Published in the United States of America
4 5 6 7 8 9 10

As always to Deidre, AJ, Amelia,
Anthony, Nick, and James

CONTENTS

Introduction

THE SINKING SHIP

Here's a story.

It was the summer of 2022, and the price of Bitcoin was hurtling downward. I mean *tanking*. Around that time, just opening my Twitter feed—or, as of a few months ago, my X feed—was like taking a walk around Pompeii in AD 79. There was screaming, crying, people predicting the end of days. Even the most optimistic investors seemed spooked.

Every few minutes, there was another long article by a financial expert declaring that the era of cryptocurrency was over. By extension, anyone who had promoted crypto at any point in the past—including, say, Italian American former White House communications directors who had taken massively long positions on financial products linked to the blockchain, thereby exposing their investors to all the ups and downs in the crypto space—seemed to be in big trouble.

So, yeah. When I got a call from a reporter at the *New York Post*'s financial section, I knew it probably wasn't for a puff piece about my favorite local brunch places. But I tried to stay cool, as usual. (Believe it or not, my one world-famous, profanity-laced phone call with a certain reporter from the *New Yorker* was not indicative of how most of my calls with reporters go. For most of my career, the press and I have gotten along swimmingly.)

I answered the phone and asked what was up.

The answer, it turned out, was *a lot*. Bitcoin was still tanking. So were a litany of other cryptocurrencies that had become popular in recent months. The reporter at the *Post* had heard that several of my clients were "eyeing the exit," which is a kind way of saying that they wanted to pull their money out of my fund and fire my ass. I took issue with some of the questions I was asked during that call, and calmly explained my point of view. If memory serves, I managed to do it without using a single curse word or accusing Steve Bannon of wanting to...uh, *fellate* himself, which I considered an achievement. But I could tell that whatever the *Post* printed tomorrow, it wasn't going to make me look like a great guy.

Whatever. I figured that after a few decades of taking shots in the press—including my eleven famous days under the watchful eye of the White House press corps, an experience that makes falling into a pit of venomous snakes seem pleasant by comparison—I would be able to take a bad write-up in the *Post* and move on without missing a beat.

The next morning, sure enough, I was right there on the landing page of the paper's website. Only it wasn't just an article. They also had a graphic of a sinking rowboat called the SS *Mooch*, of which I, the Mooch, am the captain. In the picture, my little boat is going down because it's full of heavy cartoon Bitcoins, and I'm looking toward the sky in frustration. It didn't take long before the graphic had made its way onto Twitter, then halfway around the internet, where my friends, colleagues, and occasional antagonists had some fun sharing it and writing witty captions over the top.

In a matter of hours, I had once again become a punching bag. Anyone who was getting antsy about their short-term investments in Bitcoin suddenly had someone to beat up on. So did the people who'd said crypto was a scam from the beginning. It seemed perfectly natural that the guy we could all beat up on just so happened to be the same guy who had served eleven days in the Trump White House (not ten, as has widely been reported), and was fired in shame by General John Kelly for mouthing off to a reporter.

Let's just say I've had better mornings.

During times like these, I like to take a little break from life and reflect on where I've been. Often, I'll think of all the good advice I've been given over the years from people I respect. One of the most memorable gems comes from my grandmother, a woman who knew a thing or two about hard times.

"Whatever other people think about you," she said, "it's none of your business."

Meaning: when people say bad things about you, it's none of your business, and when people say good things about you, it's *still* none of your business. The only thing you should do when times get hard is keep your head down, keep doing what you're doing, and hope that good things will come your way. If they don't, well then tough luck. Keep going.

This kind of thing is easy to say when everything is going well. But when you're taking shit from every direction—when you're on your own personal rowboat and sinking while millions of people cheer for you to go down—that kind of advice can start to sound pretty thin. It's hard to feel like something is none of your business when it's practically all you see every time you open your laptop, check your phone, or step out onto the sidewalk. Luckily, I've dealt with my fair share of failure and embarrassment over the course of my career, and it goes well beyond that single public firing you might have seen on television.

If you've followed my story up until this point, you might know the broad strokes. I was a kid from a blue-collar town on Long Island who got into Tufts University and then Harvard Law School, realizing I didn't quite belong at either one. I wore polyester to my first job interview at Goldman Sachs, then got fired from that job a few months later because I was *terrible* at it. By the time I got rehired at Goldman (wearing a regular suit this time), I had failed the New York state bar exam twice, only passing it on my third attempt. (Evidently, that's what water-skiing all summer long while your friends are home studying gets you.) From there, I quit my job to start my own companies, sold them, and ended up at the helm of SkyBridge Capital, where I remain (as of this writing, at least).

The point is, I've been around. And over the course of my career, which includes more victories, screwups, and flat-out massive mistakes than you can possibly imagine, I've learned a few lessons. One is that you should never let a relationship go sour, even if it's with someone who just fired you.

Another is that you should never use the word *granular* in a business setting. It's annoying.

But the most important lesson I've ever learned—the one that has allowed me to get up off the mat after taking some pretty intense haymakers to the jaw—is that the most important conversations you'll ever have in your life are the ones you have with yourself.

Let me put it another way. Everyone in the world has an inner voice. This is the voice that kicks in when you're about to make a big decision, or when you're at your lowest and everyone is counting you out. The most important skill you can cultivate in life is making sure that this voice—the *inner you*, so to speak—is armed with all the knowledge you can get your hands on.

When I first saw my face plastered on the homepage of the *New York Post* again, my inner voice kicked into high gear. At first, the words weren't kind.

Is this really how the world sees you? As some clown who had a big job for eleven days and will now serve as a punching bag forever?

Then I perked up. I thought about all the other times that I had been down in the dumps and sure that my career was about to take a nosedive of epic proportions. I thought about getting fired from Goldman Sachs when I was only a few years into the job. I thought about getting laughed at when I made suggestions for bad stock picks early in my career. And I thought about what happened during the 2008 financial crisis, when my company was going out of business and morale on Wall Street was at its lowest point in decades.

During that crisis, my partners and I decided to give a big middle finger to conventional wisdom and hold a big, balls-to-the-wall conference in Las Vegas—one that would soon host presidents, business leaders, and famous thinkers in all fields. To date, it is one of the most successful things we've ever done, and everyone told us it was a bad idea in the beginning.

With that in mind, I thought about my positions and reassured myself that my bets had been good. I thought back on the various lessons I've learned throughout my life about sticking it out when times get tough—lessons from my family, my friends, and the hundreds of people I've been able to meet through the SALT conference—and let out a short laugh.

A few days later, I had my assistant send the *New York Post's* graphic over to a print shop, where we had the image of me going down in the SS *Mooch* blown up, printed, and framed. As I write these words, it's hanging in my office where everyone can see it.

When people ask about the picture, I tell them it's there to remind me to have the courage of my convictions. If my investments pay off and everyone is happy with me—which is what I'm sure will happen—I'll pose beside that picture while I pop a bottle of good champagne. If the opposite happens and all my investments go to zero, I'll pop that picture off the wall, put it under my arm, and carry it out with me as I turn out the lights of SkyBridge for good.

Whatever happens, I'll know that I didn't leave anything on the field.

As of this writing, I don't know how my investment in cryptocurrency is going to turn out. It could either be one of my best ideas or the worst in the history of my career. The recent scandalous failure of the FTX exchange—a company started by someone I liked and respected, which is why I allowed them to purchase a 30-percent stake in SkyBridge—doesn't exactly make the picture look any better. In fact, the week that FTX went bust stands as one of the worst in my life.

But the good thing about being an entrepreneur is that if the worst does come to pass, I'll dust myself off and try again. If I have to go back to Port Washington, Long Island, rent a small house, and watch my beloved Mets on a television with a rabbit-ear antenna while I build the next business, I'll be happy to do it. I've got a closet full of wifebeaters that'll go great with my new lifestyle.

But there's reason to be hopeful. I think that in general, blockchain is the most innovative piece of technology to come along in centuries, right up there with the gas-powered automobile. I believe this so strongly that I've written a book on the subject, in which I point out that the ups and downs in the crypto space aren't unique; when people were first introduced to the concept of the car, many of them wondered why they would need some big, dangerous machine to do what their horse and buggy seemed to accomplish for much less money and hassle. Add that to the fact that cryptocurrencies will cut out middlemen, allow greater freedom for individuals to make purchases, and significantly reduce inflation, and I think I've got a safe bet on my hands.

But if not, I'll find something else. As Mel Brooks is once rumored to have said, we all know how this story ends. No one's getting out of here alive. So, I think it's best to take risks, keep my head down, and build as much value for my customers as possible. If I walk into a room and someone laughs at me or tells everyone I'm a loser, great. I don't care.

You might wonder where that confidence comes from. In all honesty, I'm not sure. I know it's not anything I was born with, and I certainly didn't learn it at any of the fancy schools I went to.

But thinking about it, I think I've arrived at an answer. I have been able to develop this sense of confidence and self-worth because I was raised around amazing people. I met even more amazing people when I went away to school, and even more when I struck out on my own and started my business. If there's one talent I have, it's networking, and networking is what has allowed me to learn the lessons that have kept me successful over a thirty-four-year career (one that has included many bear markets, by the way).

In recent years, that inner voice is nagging at me again.

Hey Mooch, it says. *All these people have been pretty generous with their time, and they've given you some great advice. Why not put it all in one place so the rest of the world can enjoy it, too?*

In the pages that follow, you'll find everything I know about business, life, and success. I'll cover some of the most import-ant moments in my own life—the ones that have led me to some crucial, make-or-break conversations with myself—and talk about what I think readers might be able to take from them.

More importantly, though, I'll share some of the best conver-sations I've had with *other* people, some of whom you might be familiar with. Readers will hear advice from former President Bill Clinton, General John Kelly, and the legendary investor Michael Milken. I'll talk about my conversations with Andrew Cuomo, the former governor of New York who has endured his fair share of rough patches over the past few years.

Some of these conversations have occurred onstage in front of a few hundred people at my annual SALT conference. Others have occurred in private, or on the radio. But they have all impacted my life in positive ways, and I have managed to take nuggets of wis-dom from each one. Now, I think it's time that this wisdom reaches a wider audience, which is why I have put together this book.

In this book, you will get the crash-course version of every important lesson that I have learned in my life. By the end, you'll know just about everything I know about life, business, and how to succeed. That doesn't mean you *will* succeed, of course; but it does mean that once you've reached the final page, you will be much less likely to make my mistakes.

And that would be good for everyone. Don't you think?

Prologue

DOING IT ANYWAY

There's a story about Abraham Lincoln that I've always liked, although various biographies of the man tell me that it's probably apocryphal.

It goes like this. One day, after President Lincoln had drafted the Emancipation Proclamation, he held a cabinet meeting to discuss whether he should sign it. He didn't need approval from any of the eight people in the room, but he sought it anyway. That's just the kind of guy he was, I guess. After a few minutes of arguing, the issue came to a vote. All eight of the cabinet members voted against signing the Emancipation Proclamation, which would soon free all people held as slaves in the South.

Raising his right hand, Lincoln announced the count.

"Eight nays and one aye," he said. "The ayes have it!"

During the worst of the 2008 financial crisis, I found myself in a similar position. The scale of my problems didn't quite measure up to anything President Lincoln had ever faced, but for a lowly hedge fund manager, they were major. To make a long story short, SkyBridge, the company that I had worked my ass off to build, was in trouble. Like, the going-out-of-business-any-minute-now kind of trouble. So were other major institutions on Wall Street.

Over the past few months, there had been mass layoffs. The money that these banks had been given by the federal government had come with strings. It had also come with the understanding that banks and hedge funds would have to tighten their belts, at least for a little while. As a result, most banks cancelled the conferences they'd hosted every year in places like Las Vegas. No one wanted to be seen partying while the world was burning around them.

A partner of mine had a different idea. Like me, this partner had watched all the somber faces as he walked to work each morning, and he'd felt the desperation among people on the Street. These were not the faces of people who were ready to bring the American economy back from the brink of collapse. They were people who seemed ready to wallow in their own misery forever.

He said we needed to change that, and I agreed.

Then he suggested we go to Las Vegas, hold a conference, and blow the roof off the place. Given that everyone else had already cancelled, we would be the only game in town.

At first, I thought he was nuts.

But slowly, I came around to the idea. Soon, I was downright evangelical about it. *This* was how we were going to turn things around. This was the answer.

About two months before the scheduled date for the conference, I called all five of the other SkyBridge partners into our conference room for a vote. I thought I would just pitch the idea, address a few minor concerns, ask for a vote, and count the yeses. In hindsight, I might have been a bit cocky. You have to remember, we weren't sure we'd make it through the day let alone survive to throw a bash in Vegas.

When I pitched the idea, their response was less than enthusiastic. In fact, it was downright awkward. You would have thought I was asking them to donate a kidney.

For a long time, no one would say a word.

I broke the silence.

"What's the worst that can happen?" I said, spreading my arms out and cracking a smile. "At least we'll have a going-out-of-business party!"

When it came time for the vote, I was one of two people who said yes.

Five against two.

I demurred. Then I thought of Abraham Lincoln and his cabinet meeting.

"Gentlemen, I hear your concerns," I said. "Thank you for voting. We're doing it anyway."

Two months later, we all got on planes to Las Vegas and prepared for the first annual SALT conference, SALT being short for "SkyBridge alternative." There were some bumps in the road that first year—the man calling my name introduced me as "Andy" Scaramucci at first, then "Alec"—but on the whole, the experience was positive. I spoke with the investor Michael Milken, who'd been one of my early heroes in the finance business, and met a few dozen potential clients who became good friends down the road.

Around the same time, I bought a fund-of-funds business from Citibank that turned out to be a good bet. If I had asked almost any expert in the financial world whether *that* was a good idea, they'd almost certainly have laughed in my face.

I mention these two stories right at the outset because they represent a fundamental truth: that no matter what's going on in the world, you have to trust your inner voice. You have to know when to ignore the outside world, buckle down, and make the call that you know is right.

But developing a sense of what is right and wrong isn't easy. In fact, it took me a whole lifetime of talking to people, watching people, reading books, and screwing up. By the time I made the two calls described above, I had endured plenty of failures. I had learned plenty of lessons that allowed me to develop the calluses to endure five very smart people telling me I was an idiot. That's not the kind of thing I could have done without each and every person teaching me valuable lessons.

As such, the book will begin with a tour—albeit one that is going to happen at breakneck speed—of some of those lessons.

So, let's dive in, shall we?

✎ Lesson 1

CULTIVATE JOY

*"Find ecstasy in life; the mere sense
of living is joy enough."*

—EMILY DICKINSON

There's no such thing as happiness.

Now, I'm sure you're surprised to hear me—a guy who was voted the happiest, go-luckiest asshole on Wall Street for ten years running (at least in my own mind)—say something like that. But it's true. No matter how much money you make or how many people clap when you walk into a room, you're never going to achieve a perfect state that makes you feel like you've got your life all figured out.

Anyone who's ever landed a dream job or sold the company they'd been working for years to build will tell you that this is true. Throughout my career, some of the most miserable people I've ever met have been billionaires. These guys can be standing in the middle of their own yachts, often full of people who will tell them anything they want to hear, and they'll still feel like the world is crumbling all around them. In part, that's because people who hang out on the yachts of billionaires all day tend to be...well, *suck-ups*.

But there's also a deeper element to the sadness.

The fact is that most of these sad, dejected billionaires have attached their entire sense of self-worth to their *net* worth. They believe that the more money they have, the happier they'll be. By now, it's almost a cliché to point out that this is not the case.

But I'm going to do it anyway.

There was a time in my life when I held to this same belief. When I was a law student, I believed that once I got a job at some high-end investment bank and started making a good salary—as opposed to the negative thirty thousand dollars per year I was making in law school—I would be happy. Then, once I started making the good salary at an investment bank, I started to think that if I could only leave the 9–5 job and start my own company, thereby freeing myself up to chart my own course in life and make even more money, I would be happy. I did that, and nothing changed.

This process kept going even after I had built my first business and sold it. On the evening the deal closed, my partners and I went out on the town to celebrate all we had been able to achieve. We had a fancy dinner, drank expensive wine, and told stories from the early days of the company, when everything seemed possible and we were just beginning to get our bearings in the world. But we still didn't feel any happier than we had in those first days when no one was sure if we'd be able to survive another few hours.

You know what the funniest thing about all of this is?

As all that was happening, I probably had a few hundred people tell me the same thing that I'm trying to tell you right now. Every few weeks, I would meet with someone I idolized—someone who had way more money and power than I did, and who was well respected by everyone they met, which is exactly what I wanted at the time—and they would tell me that money couldn't buy them happiness. They would tell me that once you amass enough wealth to be comfortable (as in not having to worry about paying your bills or sending your kids to college), there's no extra amount of money in the world that's going to bring you true happiness.

Once or twice, I even heard someone say, without any hint of irony, that *money doesn't buy happiness.*

I thought they were full of shit.

So, I spent a long time chasing all the expensive nonsense I could think of. I bought nice clothes, nice cars, and big houses. I used to go to dinners and blow thousands of dollars on a single check just to show people that I could.

And guess what?

The steak and the wine all tasted pretty much the same, and the feeling went away after a while. I would purchase something I'd had my eye on for a long time—a sports car, for instance, or a nice suit that had been tailored to fit my short, stocky body—and then I would get a few seconds of pleasure from the anticipation. Then, almost as quickly as it came, the feeling would go away. The happiness that I had been longing for would dissipate. That's because what I was chasing wasn't happiness in the first place, it was just material comfort.

If you're anything like I was, you probably won't take my word for it.

Luckily, you don't have to. According to Dr. Anna Lembke, a professor at Stanford University, the feelings that we call happiness and unhappiness are really the result of chemicals and neurotransmitters in our brains. The most prominent one involved in pleasure, called dopamine, is at its highest point when we're *about* to get what we want. Then, as soon as we get it, the levels go back down, and we feel a sense of pain, or emptiness. If you've ever looked at a nice pair of shoes you just blew a few hundred bucks on and suddenly felt empty and sad inside, the sudden rush of dopamine out of your brain is what you're feeling. The same goes for the sad, anxious feeling that washes over you after you just spent two hours scrolling through Instagram, hoping you'll see something interesting. When you organize your life around acquiring more and more things—even if the things in question are just momentary feelings of happiness—you'll never really feel happy.

You don't even need science to know that this is the case, although it helps. Plenty of great thinkers throughout history have known that true bliss comes from working hard and loving the small things around you. One of them was the Roman emperor Marcus Aurelius, whose book *Meditations* has been a constant source of wisdom to me throughout my life. The funny thing about this book, which even most people who've read it might not know, is that Emperor Aurelius never thought anyone was going to read it. He was just writing down thoughts that he had as he went about his days in the second century AD.

Not every one of these thoughts is applicable to your daily life. Some of them are just observations about farming, commerce, and the way bread looks when you take it out of the oven. But over the past few years, I've often found myself returning to the passages about happiness and how to achieve it. That, when it comes to the ancient philosophers, is where the good stuff is.

If you want to be a good "stoic," as followers of Marcus Aurelius and thinkers like him are often called, you can't worry about the things you can't change. That's good advice, and it's been adopted by many people over the centuries. My older brother, who's struggled with addiction for most of his adult life, heard that advice all the time during his Alcoholics Anonymous meetings. But there's a more important point, which is that you need to live in the present moment, not worrying about what everyone else is doing or what everyone else has.

Instead, you should worry about what's in front of you *right now*.

"The happiness of your life," writes Marcus Aurelius, "depends upon the quality of your thoughts: therefore, guard accordingly, and take care that you entertain no notions unsuitable to virtue and reasonable nature."

Want another one? A few years before Marcus Aurelius wrote *Meditations* or took over Rome, a man named Epictetus was born into slavery in a place called Phrygia, which is in modern-day Turkey. Despite living a life of enormous hardship—the guy's master broke his leg just for fun, leaving him crippled for the rest of his days—Epictetus managed to come to the same conclusions that Marcus Aurelius would decades later: live in the moment, focus on what you can control, and find joy in the little things; only then will you be able to achieve true joy.

For example: I'm inside right now. I'm drinking a cup of coffee. I'm looking at words on a screen that you—whoever *you* turn out be—will soon read. That might not be the kind of life they show in sexy perfume ads or write about in old folk songs, but it's a damn good life as far as I'm concerned.

You see, if you can't be happy sitting at your desk typing—or laying down tile flooring, or delivering Amazon packages, or whatever it is you get paid to do all day—you'll never be happy lounging on the deck of a yacht with champagne and supermodels. I'm sure that makes me sound insane, or like I've had a few too many glasses of champagne in my day, but it's true.

When I think of true joy, I see an image of my grandfather in the backyard of my childhood home. He's still wearing the work clothes he put on at four o'clock that morning, and the sun is beginning to set behind him. I can smell the cigarettes on his clothes and the sweet Italian liquor he's been drinking with my parents in the living room.

For the past few minutes, he's been methodically raking the lawn and placing wooden borders in a large rectangle. He's going to play bocce, an old Italian game involving pins and balls, and he's about to teach me, his grandson, how to play, too. Beside him, there are buckets of crushed-up shells from the beach near my house. When he's done laying the wooden boards for the game's border, he's going to put down a base layer of gravel and sand; then, he's going to pour the crushed shells on top of the whole thing and rake them so the surface gets nice and smooth.

If you Google "fun things to do this weekend" or "things that'll make me happy," I don't think that constructing a bocce court in your son's backyard on Long Island will be among the first few hundred results. But I've never seen anyone experience more joy from a single action than my grandfather did that night, just going through the motions his own father had taught him to construct the perfect court for a game he loved.

That was "his thing," so to speak, and it brought him joy.

Now, in this context, I'm talking about "joy" in a sense that's a little deeper than the way most people use it. I don't just mean a quick hit of positivity that comes when things start to go your way. I'm talking about the ability to step back even when things are going horribly for you and notice everything that's good about your life, no matter how small. I'm talking about cultivating the ability to take those small moments and hold them in your mind, drawing on them for the inspiration to keep going.

I remember seeing a similar sense of joy on my mother's face as she began laying out the flour, eggs, and heavy cream for a pasta recipe. I remember that she knew the whole thing by heart given how many times she'd made it, but she still read off an old three-by-five index card with her mother's handwriting on it. I've seen it on the faces of guys who used to collect baseball cards when they come across one on eBay that they would have loved when they were a kid, and I've seen it on the faces of people listening to a song they love on the radio.

Does this sound stupid yet? I'm sure it does. But I've found that when it comes to abstract things like happiness and living a good life, there's a very fine line between stupid and profound. That is: if you've heard something a million times, read it in every book about how to live well, and heard some crypto entrepreneur clown repeat it on every podcast you tune into, that might just be because it's true.

In this case, the true thing that you've heard a million times is that money will not buy you happiness. I know it sounds like a cliché, but it's true. What *will* bring you happiness, however, is cultivating joy in your life—noticing the small things that make you happy and learning to appreciate them. If you can learn to love the experience of being alive, to love your family, and to love the time you spend with your friends, you'll end up being happy in whatever else you choose to do.

Take me, for instance. I've got more money than most people. For a long time, I organized my entire life around the pursuit of more money. But I also learned the hard way that focusing only on your work and the acquisition of more material wealth isn't going to get you anywhere; always searching for the next thing is only going to make you want more things.

The human brain is a dangerous thing in that way. If you don't believe me, check out some of the best writers in the history of the English language. Writing in *Paradise Lost*, his epic poem about the fall of man, John Milton has Satan (who, if you can believe it, is the hero of the story) proclaim that "The mind is its own place, and in itself can make a heaven of a hell or a hell of a heaven." William Shakespeare, who also knew a thing or two about human nature, said that "There is nothing either good or bad but thinking makes it so."

In other words, learn to notice the small things that make you happy, and you'll find true happiness. Material things will not get you there. Trust me. Right now, my hedge fund has a huge crypto exposure, and that market (as I've found out over the past couple of years) is not exactly stable, despite what some of the people pushing it might want to tell you. There is risk inherent in investing in something so new and revolutionary, just like there is a certain amount of risk in everything.

But if all my accounts go to zero tomorrow—and thanks to the crypto exposure, they might—I'll be fine going back to my house, cracking open a can of Schlitz with my buddies, and watching my beloved New York Mets play on my old rabbit-eared television (if I can still get a good signal off the Empire State Building). As long as I have my family, I'll have joy.

And there is nothing more important than joy.

Learn to recognize it and cultivate it in yourself, and you'll be able to deal with anything that life or business throw your way.

BEWARE OF YOUR EGO

*"If you can't swallow your pride,
you can't lead."*

—GENGHIS KHAN

This book is going to include a lot of lessons. That's kind of the point. In some cases, I'm not much more qualified than the next person to impart these little pearls of wisdom. I'm sure, for instance, that there have been times when I've failed to feel joy at the small things in the way I just told you to. I'm also not the world's leading expert in any of the books I'll be discussing, and I don't have any kind of advanced degree in history or science. Even my knowledge of finance, when you really get down to the gritty details, is limited compared to some people I know (some of whom, thank God, work for me).

But when it comes to ego and the dangers it holds, I might as well be Albert fucking Einstein.

Throughout my life, I've made a great deal of terrible decisions because of my ego. (I've made some good ones, too, but everyone gets lucky occasionally.) In that time, I've learned that there is no more dangerous force on planet earth than your ego.

If you're looking for a definition of this word that I've now used four times, and will use again before this lesson is over, look no further than the Greek playwright Aeschylus, who wrote often about human frailty and hubris. In the beginning of most of his plays, Aeschylus included the phrase, *Obtia obia nemesis*, which translates roughly to "My pride and my ego are my enemy."

It's also the one-word answer that I give to people when they ask me how in the hell—although most of my friends don't say "hell"—I ended up going to work for Donald J. Trump, the sleaziest, saddest, most run-down low life ever to occupy the Oval Office, when he managed to get elected president.

Ego.

But since this is a book, and we have the room to "dig deep," as a therapist might say, allow me to explain.

When I was young, my parents had nothing. While I would never disrespect my father's work ethic by saying we grew up poor, it's clear looking back that we didn't enjoy the material comforts that come with having a lot of money. There were weeks when we ate light dinners, and there were summers when we left the air conditioners off through some blisteringly hot nights just to save a little money on electricity. It was hard not to notice that we were struggling.

In several books and speeches, I've told the story of how that experience shaped me as a person. Hell, I just told it to *you* a few pages ago. But I've never talked about the extent to which providing for my family at such a young age let me develop a massive (and, some would say unhealthy) ego.

In a sense, I needed that ego to survive. Every time I climbed on my bike and started delivering papers or clocked into my job at the grocery store, I was building myself up, telling myself that I was the guy who could make things happen for my family. I was going to work my ass off, and nothing was going to stop me.

Fast-forward a few years, and I was a full-blown workaholic. I was also, though it pains me to admit it, completely addicted to status. Every time I told someone I was going to Tufts University or Harvard Law School, there'd be a small glint in their eye that made me feel like I was doing something worthwhile. I knew that those were good schools, and I knew that people were impressed by me attending them. When I was seventeen, I even turned down an offer from a much cheaper public college on the grounds that Tufts was a more prestigious university (and one that, presumably, could offer me a much better education). That ego-driven quest for status continued as I made my way through some of the most elite circles in the country: Wall Street, Republican politics, the media, and any other cool-sounding place I could get into.

The only place left to go, it seemed, was the White House.

So, when I was finally offered a place by President Trump, I did what I and many other people had been doing for just over two years. I overlooked his massive shortcomings—the racism, the attitude, and the earth-shattering stupidity—because I wanted a chance to play with the big kids and go to work every day at 1600 Pennsylvania Avenue. I wanted to have drinks at the Trump hotel in town, pal around with reporters, and generally be part of the crowd that shaped global events rather than just watching them and making financial decisions based on them.

More than anything, I wanted my mother to be able to tell her friends that her son was working at the White House. For decades, I'd been trying to impress my mother, who wasn't always the easiest woman in the world to please. I've often told the story that when I got a job at Goldman Sachs straight out of Harvard

Law School, she went around telling her friends that Goldman was a law firm; she didn't know what the bank actually did, but she couldn't stand the fact that I wasn't a lawyer.

So, yeah. I took a job in the White House in part because I wanted my mother to be proud of me. And it worked. On the day that I became the communications director, she went down to the corner store and bought a big stack of every newspaper they had, adorning her living room with about two dozen images of my face, which happened to be on the front page that day. To this day, I'm not sure if I've ever seen that woman prouder of me—and it's not exactly like I'd been lying around doing nothing up until that point.

Maybe that's why I decided to take the job despite so many obvious red flags. One of the most obvious, of course, was that my wife told me in no uncertain terms she would seriously consider filing for divorce if I took the job. She was pregnant at the time, and the last thing she needed was me taking a job that was going to have me working even longer hours than I was already working.

She also couldn't stand the president, which was understandable. You might even say that my first job as Trump's communications director was getting my wife to like the guy, or at least to stop thinking he should be exiled to Siberia and fed to hungry tigers.

I failed at that, by the way, which should have been an indication of things to come.

But it wasn't. When you're dealing with your ego, you'd be amazed how many obstacles and red flags you can ignore.

About three days after I accepted the job, I found myself sitting aboard Air Force One with President Trump and the rest of the goon squad. We had Kellyanne Conway, Stephen Miller, and a few traveling press aides who looked like little members of the Hitler Youth in cheap, ill-fitting suits. I hadn't yet begun to wonder why the hell I was wasting so much time working with a group of people that so obviously stood for the opposite of what I did on so many issues, but I was close.

As we touched down in West Virginia, the notion that I had just begun to make a big mistake dawned on me. Sitting there with the president of the United States, giving my counsel, and helping to shape global issues in the way I had always wanted to, I felt a familiar feeling of emptiness and regret, though only for a moment. (You tend to forget things when you're moving eighty miles a minute trying to prepare for a big speech, and to keep yourself from getting wrapped up in whatever crime this big orange dummy is going to commit next.)

Still, there on the tarmac, I began to understand that my ego, and my desire to do a big job for the cameras, may have led me way off course.

Maybe it's because my wife was sitting at that very moment in a hospital bed in New York, preparing to give birth to our second child. We had talked about the possibility that this might happen, of course. Her due date was only a few weeks after I was supposed to get back from the trip, and I knew from my previous four children that babies come early sometimes. If I'd been the devoted husband I should have been, I would have stayed home and taken care of my wife on the off chance that she went into labor a little sooner than expected.

But I didn't.

Now, I'm sure that if this were a screenplay, this is when the director would hand it back to the writer and give some notes. *Come on*, he might say. *The guy's not really going to miss the birth of his child because he wants to go work in the White House to please his own fragile ego, is he? No one's that much of a schmuck. The audience just won't buy it. Do a page-one rewrite on this "Mooch" guy, stat.*

Sadly, this was real life.

At the time, I made myself feel a little better by speaking to a few buddies who'd spent time overseas in the Army and the Marines. They told me that they'd missed the birth of some of their children because they were in Afghanistan defending their country. They said that they'd all been called to serve just like I had, and sometimes service means sacrificing the things you love. Looking back on those conversations now, I can see they're a load of shit. But they made me feel a little better at the time.

The irony of the whole situation, of course, is that my quest to satiate my ego ended up doing exactly the opposite. After a few choice words on the phone with a reporter from the *New Yorker* that I probably don't need to repeat here—you can Google it if you managed to buy this book without knowing *that* whole story—I got thrown out onto Pennsylvania Avenue on my ass, then rolled in margarita salt so the cuts and bruises stung as much as possible. Every late-night comedian in the country made jokes about me. I was impersonated on *Saturday Night Live* by Bill Hader, who slicked his hair back and wore the biggest pinky ring you've ever seen for the occasion.

Sitting here writing these words, I can still see some of the worst headlines.

(Again, you can Google these.)

Now, I did eventually work myself out of that deep hole. But when I was actually *in* the hole, having just about everyone in the world laughing at me, it wasn't clear whether I was ever going to be able to get out again. Things seemed pretty dark, and I knew that

I had only managed to get myself into this bad situation because I didn't have my priorities straight. My priorities, such as they were, involved nothing more than making sure I gained as much status and attention as possible. I wanted to serve my government, but I wanted to do it for the wrong reasons, which is why I was so willing to sign up to serve a president who was so manifestly unqualified for the job.

I was doing everything to gratify my own ego. And when you find yourself doing that, you need to make a change right away, because it's only a matter of time before it comes back to bite you. That's just the kind of sense of humor that God has. If you attach all your self-worth to your image, sitting in front of the mirror for hours so you can gratify yourself by looking better than everyone else (something I've never suffered from), you can bet that your appearance is going to be the first thing to go. If your drug is money, then eventually you're either going to lose it all, or you're going to find out that it doesn't bring you anywhere near the satisfaction you were looking for.

In the early twentieth century, a mythologist named Joseph Campbell published a series of essays on mythology and narrative called *The Hero with a Thousand Faces*. If you've never read it, I would highly suggest that you do. You'll find that he's not writing only about old works of Shakespeare and the Greek tragedians, but just about every movie and television show you've ever seen. Many of these shows, you might realize, involve what Campbell calls "the hero's journey," a common plot device that has been used in everything from the *Epic of Gilgamesh* to modern television shows such as *The Wire* and *Game of Thrones*.

Although it takes different forms, the hero's journey usually involves a few stages. First, the hero is called to action. The town gets together and asks a young knight, for instance, to go on a quest. In most cases, the hero refuses at first. (Incidentally, this is exactly what happened when President Trump first asked me to join his board of advisors shortly after being elected; I said no, he laughed, and then he announced on television that I was joining anyway, much to my chagrin.) Then, for the rest of the story, the hero enters an unfamiliar world, crossing the threshold from the life he's known into something new, dark, and challenging; by the end of this process, he's undergone something that Campbell calls "ego death."

Now, I'm not saying that I'm the hero of the story I just told you. At eleven days, I'm not even sure that the events of the story would fill a pamphlet, let alone a full book. But I sure as hell experienced "ego death," (which, as it turns out, feels like getting dragged behind an eighteen-wheeler over broken glass). According to Campbell, ego—or the attachment to a certain set of beliefs about yourself—is there to maintain order and stability, but it can come at the cost of personal growth and spiritual development. To achieve ego death, one must go through a transformative experience that challenges their preconceptions and beliefs, leading to a complete dissolution of the self. This process can be difficult and painful, but it is necessary for individuals to connect with something greater than themselves and achieve a deeper understanding of the universe.

Now, I don't know if I understand much more about the universe than I did before I went to work in the White House, but my ego has definitely taken a hit. That, at least, is a good thing. It's taught me that self-gratification is a very bad reason to take a job or begin a new venture. So is the hope that you might impress people by doing whatever you're about to do.

Like so much in this book, (I hope), I went through the pain—and the hero-but-not-really-a-hero hero's journey—so that you don't have to.

You're welcome.

Lesson 3

OWN YOUR MISTAKES

"There are no mistakes here,
just happy accidents."

—Bob Ross

This book started with a low point in my career.

Here's another one. It was November of 2022, and I had just arrived in the Bahamas, where I had a meeting scheduled with Sam Bankman-Fried from FTX. I'd heard rumors that Sam was using client money to fund risky trades, which is a big no-no in the world of finance. I had come down to this tropical paradise for a heart-to-heart with him and a few associates to see if we could still make the deal work.

I was hoping he would tell me that the whole thing had been a misunderstanding—that everyone was wrong, that the books were fine, and that the exchange was healthy.

He didn't.

I pieced the facts together and arrived at the truth, which was that the financial health of FTX was about as good as Donald J. Trump's *actual* health. There were big holes in the books, money was missing, and no one knew quite what was going on. I didn't want to use the word "fraud" at the time—and I still don't, given the legal implications—but it was only a matter of time before the whole thing would come crashing down.

At some point, I took the general counsel of the company outside for a walk. He was a nice kid, just a few years out of law school. I could tell that he was as shocked by Sam's behavior as I was. When we got outside, he started telling me about what he knew. Then he stopped, looking about as worried as I've ever seen anyone.

"What should I do?" he said.

In the two or three seconds that it took me to answer, I drew on about five decades of lessons. I thought back to conversations I've had, books I've read, and stories that I've heard secondhand. They all pointed to the same answer.

"Tell the truth," I said. "Tell everyone exactly what happened. You're a young guy, and you can rebuild your career after this. If you didn't know about it, then say that. But you've got to tell the truth."

The next morning, he resigned and tipped off the Securities and Exchange Commission and the Department of Justice about what was going on. As of this writing, the company remains under investigation. If you've been following the news, you can probably guess that the findings aren't going to be good. But whatever happens, that young lawyer will be able to live the rest of his life knowing that he did the right thing. Unlike some people who worked at FTX, he'll be able to look people in the eye knowing he was honest and forthright when it counted.

Now, you might think that I was just delivering what I thought sounded like good advice—something I learned in a book somewhere or picked up on a podcast.

Sadly, that's not the case.

Throughout the course of my life, I've made some horrific mistakes, and I've learned how to react when it seems like the whole world is about to come crashing down on my head.

Fortunately, the way you're supposed to react when you've made a big mistake is the same no matter what situation you're in. First, identify who's in charge. This is an easy step, because it's usually the person you'll picture throwing you off a fiftieth-floor balcony for screwing up as bad as you did.

That's normal.

Step two is to tell that person and work out a plan.

Sometimes, though, there's no one in charge. Sometimes, you find yourself in the situation that my friend, the FTX lawyer, was in—when the guy who was supposed to be in charge turns out to be a liar, a fraud, or a creep (or all three), and you've got to figure out the next steps in the process on your own.

Luckily, I've got stories that apply to both situations.

It was 1991. I was twenty-seven years old, fresh out of Harvard Law School and working on the trading desk at Goldman Sachs. In terms of my inner life, I was swinging from massive insecurity to extreme overconfidence, bordering on arrogance. That's when a young biotechnology analyst at the firm alerted me to the existence of a company called Centocor.

Centocor, according to this analyst's research, was developing a new blockbuster drug that was going to cure sepsis and drastically reduce mortality in hospitals. Sepsis, you might know, is a terrible affliction. We still don't have a cure for it. But after meeting with the analyst for a few minutes, I decided I was a genius. Despite having no medical degree or experience in biotechnology, I was going to become Goldman Sach's new biotech expert in residence, and my first big bet was on Centocor's new drug.

I bought call options leading into the Food and Drug Administration (FDA) phase one approval for the drug and waited for news. If it was good news, I stood to make a whole lot of money.

A few days later, the worst possible thing happened.

The FDA approved the drug, and my call options went from being worth around $6,000 to more than $80,000.

Now, I could have used that money to pay off my law school debt or invest in some more suits that weren't shiny and highly flammable. But I didn't. I had made one good call in the biotech space, and suddenly the high opinion that I had of myself had been validated.

I took my earnings and "rolled them into" the forward call sequence for the phase two trials, believing that the drug was destined for market and that I couldn't lose.

I believed it so much, in fact, that I flew to Washington, DC— like, on a plane and everything—and sat in the hearing room awaiting approval for the drugs. Sitting there, watching the Washington bureaucrats pore over the research, I felt like the smartest guy in the world. I was already dreaming up all the stupid shit I was going to buy when my positions grew tenfold and made me millions.

Then the announcement came. Not only was the approval not coming; they had revoked their previous approval, meaning that even my previous earnings—the ones that had made me believe I was an expert in the first place—were effectively worthless. Because of some intricacies in the way the deal was structured, my account had a negative balance of $50,000. I was about to cost the firm about $50,000, all because I thought I was an expert in a field that I wasn't.

This was a big mistake—the kind that gets you a talking-to from your boss and a nice cardboard box for your personal items.

I had no idea what to do.

But something kicked in, and for the first time that week, I managed to do the right thing. I walked into my boss's office and told him exactly what happened. I didn't try to blame anyone else or make excuses. I said that I had fucked up big-time, and that we were all in trouble because of me.

Now, he wasn't thrilled to hear this news. But his reaction was a whole lot better than it would have been if I had, say, tried to hide my losses and make them up in secret with another bright idea in the biotech space (which, you won't be surprised to learn, is no longer my forte). In the end, he said that he would cover what I had lost on the deal, and that the company would dock my paycheck a few hundred dollars every week until it had its money back.

So, along with my $100,000 of law school debt, I had another fifty grand of what you might call "dumbass payments" to make every week, too. That was a hole that I didn't climb out of for a long time. But once I did, I had a full understanding of how much a bad trade can take from you. I had also learned the horrible things that can happen when you get too far over your skis, expertise-wise.

So, that's a time when I did the right thing after making a huge, potentially career-ending mistake. There is, of course, an alternate version of my life where I did the wrong thing—when I kept doubling down and trying to hide my mistake until I was a few million in the hole rather than fifty thousand. You would think that after narrowly escaping that fate, I would have been especially attuned to the dangers of not coming right out and admitting your mistakes at the first possible opportunity.

But I wasn't.

When I left the White House, I stayed quiet for a long time.

Well, not *quiet.* I guess you can't really apply that word to anyone who went on a dozen different talk shows, spoke publicly about the experience often, and then wrote an entire book about the experience.

But I did stay quiet about what mattered, which is the fact that I spent eleven days working for a guy who never should have become president in the first place. In fact, the book that I wrote about my very short time in the White House made the case that President Trump was actually *better* qualified for the job than people might have thought. (That book, incidentally, is still widely available, and I've got a few hundred copies in my basement if anyone wants to purchase them instead of firewood this winter.)

There were many things in that book that I believed. But there were certainly places where I was lying to myself about what I had been part of. Whenever I went on television to claim that we were not, in fact, in a massive amount of trouble with President Trump at the helm of our country, I was trying to cover up one of the biggest mistakes I had ever made. Rather than coming forward the day after—or even the week or the month after—I ran around, tried to get my company back on track, and hoped that I would never have to address what I had done wrong. I hoped I would be able to avoid the consequences of my mistake forever and that the world would just move on, beginning to see me as the kindly Italian American hedge fund manager who showed up on television sometimes, *not* the guy who used to work for the worst president in recent memory.

That was never going to happen.

At some point, President Trump attacked me on Twitter after I had said something mildly negative about him. The timing doesn't matter very much, nor does what he said. I just remember sitting in my kitchen, getting the message, and knowing I was going to have to respond with something twice as brutal as he'd given me. I did that, and we traded barbs back and forth for a while. But even then, I wasn't ready to really look at what I'd done and publicly apologize for it. I still told people that the president and I might have a better relationship someday, and that I was rooting for him to succeed.

Again, it wasn't true. I was still hiding.

Now, some of you might call me a liar when you read this. But you should remember that every day, we all lie a little to ourselves, and sometimes we live in denial. If you understand the human condition, you know that self-deception is part of all of us.

We all lie to ourselves.

Today, when I hit the speaking circuit and mention my distaste for my former boss, there are still people who tell me I waited too long to say something. There are also people who assume, not without reason, that I waited to speak out until President Trump attacked me, meaning that my whole act is self-interested.

Unfortunately, I don't have much to rebut that. All I can do is show you what happens when you do the wrong thing and tell you that the consequences are not worth failing to speak out. Many people who served in that administration did the same as me. They knew that they did something wrong working for Trump, yet they still cannot admit it. Therefore, they are taking a different path away from the truth.

When you do something wrong, admit it, and do it fast. The comfort you get in the short term from avoiding that pain is always going to go away, and the pain, when it does come, is going to kick your ass.

There's a small chance that as you were reading this section, something flashed through your mind. Maybe it's something you've been feeling guilty about for a long time—a small mistake at work that you were hoping no one would notice, or a series of lies you've told that you've been hoping won't get you into trouble down the line.

I'm sure this is the last thing you want to hear, but it's time to do something about it.

The best time to own up to what you did was right after it happened. The second-best time is now.

So, go ahead.

(I'm serious. Call your boss. Send the dreaded email. This book will be here when you get back.)

LEARN TO LAUGH
AT YOURSELF

"Wow, the White House is great!
I'm going to work here for a long time."

—ANTHONY SCARAMUCCI

If you've seen *Back to the Future*, you might know an actor named Michael J. Fox. As a young, Republican-leaning kid on Long Island, I used to relate to his character on *Family Ties*, in which he played a straitlaced, conservative young man named Alex P. Keaton, who wore nice clothes and loved Ronald Reagan. Today, he might be best known for running the Michael J. Fox Foundation, which raises money to cure Parkinson's disease, an affliction Fox has struggled with (often in the public eye) for decades now.

But before all that, he was a young actor trying to make his mark on Hollywood.

And he was short.

For most guys looking to break into the business—to become the next James Bond or Indiana Jones—that might have been a reason to quit. In the early 1980s, no one was used to action stars, or even comedians, who were shorter than five-foot-four-and-a-half, as he was. At the very least, it might have been something that Fox tried to hide. He could have demanded that directors shoot his coverage in a way that made him look more physically imposing, (which, if you believe the rumors, is exactly what his near contemporary Tom Cruise was fond of doing).

Instead, he leaned into it. He took roles for short guys, and made up for what he lacked in height by being charming, personable, and hilarious. Even when the material wasn't great, his delivery was. And when Fox won awards for those roles—which he often did—he'd run up on stage and make a joke about how the microphone wasn't low enough for him. Before long, the first thing you noticed about the guy wasn't his short stature or how physically unimposing he was; it was how great of an actor he was.

By the time *Back to the Future Part III* came out and made an entire generation of young men want to be cowboys all over again, Fox had become one of the biggest stars on the planet, largely because he knew how to laugh at himself.

Most importantly, he knew how to do it right away, before anyone else had a chance to do it for him. By doing so, he put the people around him at ease. He let them know that they didn't have to hide their comments about his height or pretend it wasn't a factor. Sometimes, one quick joke is all it takes to make people feel comfortable around you. It lets people know that you're not going to get upset if they criticize you, and that you're comfortable enough in your own skin to take jokes and mean comments in stride.

We all know people who can't do this. I'm sure I'm not the only one who, before being led into a room to meet someone new, is told by an associate of that person *not* to mention the one thing they're insecure about, be it a mole, a toupee, or an embarrassing incident from their past. Right off the bat, this makes everyone in the room feel tense. It also makes people inherently distrustful.

They might start asking questions. *If this guy is insecure about that*, they wonder, *what else should I avoid saying*?

This is a bad way to do business. It's a bad way to live your life in general. Over the course of nearly six decades on earth, I've found that cracking a quick joke about the thing you're insecure about—even if you're deeply insecure about it—is much better than trying to dance around it forever.

Think about me. Do you think there's a single room I've walked into since August of 2017 that wasn't filled with people who watched me flame out in horrific fashion on national television? Probably not! And even if they didn't know before I walked in there, they sure as hell knew by the time I walked out. That's because I say it first, long before anyone else can make their stupid joke about working for Trump. Flip back through this book, and you'll probably see two or three times that I've done it already.

And speaking of that guy, has there ever been a person who is less able to joke about himself? Who makes people *more* tense and uncomfortable when they're in a room with him because they're afraid of saying the wrong thing? I mean, this is a guy who literally sued Bill Maher, a comedian, for claiming that he was the product of a sex act between an adult woman and an orangutang. In the 1980s, when Trump got wind of an article in *Spy* magazine that called him a "short-fingered vulgarian," he immediately took to the press to correct the record. For the next several decades, he worked in the length of his fingers—as well as his height, his wealth, and how smart he was—into every interview and conversation he had.

Trust me. I've known the guy a long time.

Not only is this kind of thing embarrassing, but it's also a waste of time. You're never going to make people *not* notice something about you that they think is funny or embarrassing. No matter how hard you try, you can't make bad things go away just by talking, or by intimidating people into pretending they don't exist.

Even if you're the most secure person in the world—which you might be—I guarantee you that eventually, you'll become deeply insecure about something. You'll do something stupid in public that someone will get on film, and you'll become the "main character of Twitter" for a few days. You might say something to someone at a party that goes over horribly, giving the rest of the people who were at that party a gossipy story to tell for the next few months.

Whatever it is, try to understand that making it go away will only make it worse. Pushing the bad thing down will cause it to fester and grow more poisonous inside you. It's much better to get it all out in the open.

Like anything else, this is a skill you can cultivate. When you learn to laugh off the little things you don't like about yourself— whether it's your bad style or the way you speak—you'll be ready when the big thing comes. Maybe the big thing will be an embarrassing social faux pas like the ones I described above. Maybe you'll just mouth off to a reporter, get fired, and get mocked for a few days.

Or maybe it'll be much more serious than that.

Consider what happened to Fox, a guy who learned the power of laughing at himself very early in life, when he turned twenty-nine years old. Around that time, he was diagnosed with Parkinson's disease, a serious and often fatal condition that affects the central nervous system in devastating ways. At first, people who get Parkinson's notice that they're having trouble focusing

Shortly thereafter, the physical symptoms begin. People notice that they can't quite perceive depth the way they used to, and their limbs begin shaking. It's not long before these people lose control of their bodies almost completely; their arms will fly in all directions, their head will turn to either side rapidly, and their shoulders will go up and down at will.

In other words, the disease makes people shake in a way that's impossible for other people not to notice. For an actor, especially one whose comic timing depends on being in complete control of the face and body, the diagnosis would be devastating. It would give a weak person more than enough reason to retire from public life completely. Aside from the obvious difficulties that come with Parkinson's disease—primarily the inability to get around or communicate effectively—there is always the danger that people are going to laugh at you.

I'm not saying these are good people. But they exist. Do a quick Google search for "Michael J. Fox Parkinson's funny," and you'll find several entries dedicated to telling crude, dark jokes about the guy. You'll see that the animated series *Family Guy* has done segments in which Fox is portrayed as a shaking, incompetent idiot. You might also find a clip from a few years ago in which the right-wing radio host Rush Limbaugh gets a good ten minutes out of mocking Fox for the way he shook during his congressional testimony about the need to make Parkinson's drugs more affordable.

To most people, getting that kind of negative attention—not to mention the disease itself—would be a perfect excuse to sit back, rest, and stay out of the game forever. Given how many successful films and television shows he'd made by the time he got diagnosed, Fox could have done that with ease. He could have stayed quiet, hoping that the jokes would stop and that people would feel bad for him.

But he didn't.

Instead, he came right out and kept on cracking jokes about himself, even when the subject matter had become deadly serious. For a while, he had a sitcom in which he played himself, Parkinson's and all. In 2011, he even appeared on an episode of *Curb Your Enthusiasm* in which he made many great jokes at his own expense.

The scene was not only hilarious, but also cathartic. As humans, we like seeing people who can take terrible circumstances and make them seem surmountable. We also like people who are secure enough in themselves that they can smile, joke around, and have a laugh at the very things that you'd think make them insecure.

You might wonder where Fox found the strength to do that. He gives us a clue in an introductory essay that he wrote when his second memoir, *Always Looking Up*, came out. In his words, we can see a perfect encapsulation of the guy's worldview.

"As the title for this new book," he writes, "*Always Looking Up* works on a couple of levels."

First off—let's just get this one out of the way—it's a short joke. At a fraction of an inch under five-foot-five, much of my interaction with the world and the people in it has required that I tilt my head backward and direct my gaze upward. However, this isn't a manifesto about the hardships of the vertically challenged. Frankly, my height or lack thereof never bothered me much. Although there's no doubt that it's contributed to a certain mental toughness. I've made the most of the head start one gains from being underestimated. And that's more to the point of it—*Always Looking Up* alludes to an emotional, psychological, intellectual, and spiritual outlook that has served me throughout my life and, perhaps, even saved me throughout my life with Parkinson's. It's not that I don't feel the aching pain of loss. Physical strength, spontaneity, physical balance, manual dexterity, the freedom to do the work I want to do when I want to do it, the confidence that I can always be there for my family when they need me—all of these have been, if not completely lost to Parkinson's, at least drastically compromised.

In the book, which I'd encourage everyone to read, Fox gives great advice about how to get through hard times. He describes scenarios that would be difficult for most people to imagine. During some of the worst public embarrassments I've ever endured, I always made a point to wake up, look at the sunrise, and thank God that I still had my family and my health. As guys like Fox can tell you, it's hard to imagine what *not* having your health is like until you don't.

But there are ways to endure even those horrible trials. As Fox writes, you do this by separating the things you can't control—like having Parkinson's disease—from the things you *can* control. You stop freaking out about the first thing, and you put all your energy into the second thing. Rather than letting your affliction consume you and become your identity, you focus on faith, family, and creativity.

Reading that, it's hard to imagine that anyone wants to make fun of this guy's condition. But we live in a world full of shitty people—the kind who thrive on making others feel weak and small, whose only comfort in life is picking on people to get a cheap laugh.

There are a few ways to get back at people like this. One is to give it right back to them. I know I've done that more than a few times.

But in the end, fighting back in that way tends to leave you feeling empty. We also have too much of it right now. A few months ago, I had the pleasure of interviewing Mark Esper, the man who served as President Trump's secretary of defense during some of the most tumultuous months our country has ever experienced. At some point during that podcast, he lamented the tendency of people in our political system to resort to name-calling and petty partisan squabbling over substantive conversations.

Politics, and life in general, he says, is now "marked by incivility, name-calling, and getting down in the mud with people who want to go there...And I just don't want to go there."

This is smart. Which is why the other option—killing the people who hate you with kindness, making the same joke they were going to make, or, preferably, an even better one—is always a better option.

I'm sorry if I'm the first one to tell you this, but here it is: You can't stop other people from laughing at you. It's just not going to happen. If there's something funny about you—whether it's your height, your weight, your voice, or the way you dress—people are going to notice, and the worst among them are going to mock you for it.

That might not be nice, but that's the way the world works. If they can do it to Michael J. Fox—by all accounts a first-ballot,

Hall-of-Fame great guy who is suffering from a serious medical condition—they'll definitely do it to you.

They've even done it to a (sort of) nice guy like me. As I've written about before, when I first showed up on the campus of Tufts University, I stood out like a sore thumb. At the time, I was still wearing the clothes that made me feel cool on Long Island: leather motorcycle jackets, boots, gold chains, etc. Most of the kids I passed on campus were nice about my dorky outfit. At least they didn't mention it. Some weren't so nice. There was a time when that might have upset me a lot. (Like, when I was six years old.) I would have gone home, snuggled up with my black leather blankie, and cried myself to sleep.

Luckily, though, I grew up with my grandmother, whose age-old wisdom was drilled into me from a young age.

What other people think about you is none of your business.

Did I already use that one?

Well, I don't care, because it's one of the foundational phrases of my life. If you want a little variety, here's the ancient philosopher Marcus Aurelius—who has also appeared in these pages already, and for good reason—saying a variation on the same thing in his book *Meditations*.

"I have often wondered," he writes, "how it is that every man loves himself more than all the rest of men, but yet sets less value on his own opinion of himself than on the opinions of others."

Later he writes, "How much time he gains who does not look to see what his neighbor says or does or thinks, but only at what he does himself, to make it just and holy."

Although I was still a few months away from encountering the work of Marcus Aurelius for the first time when I showed up at Tufts in my mismatched outfit, I felt like I'd been taking his words to heart for years. (Thanks, Nona.) When I was in fourth grade, I attended my first day of gym class to find a cranky, old man teaching named Alfred Wagner,[i] who hated kids with long, Italian names. He wasn't a fan of the Irish either, whose names had just as many vowels on the beginnings of their names as we Italians had on the end. Mr. Wagner, by his own admission, preferred Smiths, Johnsons, and Petersons. No ethnic funny business.

So, he gave nicknames to the kids with immigrant parents— monosyllabic things that he could scream across the gym and get our attention.

Mine was "Mooch."

There were some kids who hated their nicknames. I certainly did. They felt the gym teacher was mocking their heritage, singling them out for scorn because of something they had no control over. When you're a kid, and gym class is one of the most important things you've ever done in your life, this can damage your sense of self in major ways. It can even make you want to please the cranky, old guy who's making fun of your name, hoping that if you do what he wants all the time, he might stop making fun of you.

Luckily, I'd been raised right. So, I took a different approach.

Rather than hiding from the guy and always wondering what he thought about me, I started going by "Mooch" among my friends. I knew that I couldn't control what this guy thought of me, and so I didn't try to change it. Instead, I decided to focus on my reaction to what he called me, which was completely within my control.

I'm not saying it worked wonders for me. The guy was still a pain in the ass and vaguely bigoted towards ethnic kids, (especially the ones who didn't seem to be all that afraid of him). But I got to walk into gym class every day knowing that this guy didn't

---

i   For obvious reasons, this man's name has been changed to protect the guilty.

have any power over me. I didn't try to change my behavior to make him like me because I knew he was never going to. Instead, I embraced everything he was throwing my way and tried to turn a negative into a positive.

That was under my control. Everything else was not.

To this day, people still call me Mooch. If you and I ever meet in the street, you're more than welcome to do so. I've been using the name for so long, in fact, that I've almost forgotten it was once something a cranky, old gym teacher on Long Island used to make fun of me. And let's face it: I have been called a lot worse.

Which, I guess, is the point.

So, to summarize: There's a good way to deal with shortcomings, especially in a business setting, and that is to beat everyone to the punch. Got something you're insecure about? Great. *You* say it, preferably in a way that shows everyone in the room that you can laugh at yourself. That way everyone feels at ease around you, feels they can trust you, and everyone starts the relationship off on the right foot.

If you've seen the movie *8 Mile*, a slightly fictionalized account of the rise of the rapper Eminem, you've seen this in action. Toward the end of the film, Eminem gets up and performs a freestyle rap that cuts deep. He lays in everything that people were about to make fun of him for, thereby rendering all further insults moot. There was nothing left for his opponents to say about him.

Learn to do that now, while the stakes are low, because someday you might not have a choice.

Take my situation, for instance. When I was kicked out of the White House on my ass, I didn't have the ability to make the joke before anyone else. Every comedian in the country, from losers on Twitter to professionals, had already kicked the shit out of me.

This is the kind of experience that would have crippled someone who had spent their life up to that point trying to avoid pain. For someone who had been focused on nothing but what other people think—who had organized their life to avoid being called names or made fun of—the kind of public shaming I endured would have been career ending.

For me, it wasn't.

That's not because I'm superhuman or because I have access to some secret knowledge that most people don't have. It's simply because I had been building up my self-mockery muscles for decades by the time most Americans even knew who I was. There was no joke that any late-night comedian could make about me that I wasn't just as willing to make about myself.

As a result, most people don't hate me. I'm not saying anyone loves me or anything, because there are plenty of examples of people who still attack me relentlessly whenever I step out in public. But because I didn't shy away from the jokes and the scorn—because I actively contributed to those things, in some cases—I've been able to weather the storm well. I'm back at the helm of SkyBridge, and I host a podcast about things that interest me. I've written another book with all the advice I've picked up over the course of my career, and you happen to be holding that book right now.

I mean, you wouldn't have bought this book if I were just some loser who got fired from the White House after eleven days and then cut a bad deal with some floppy-haired crypto kid, right?

Right?

BE OPTIMISTIC

*"Optimism is a strategy for making a better
future. Because unless you believe that the
future can be better, you are unlikely to step
up and take responsibility for making it so."*

—Noam Chomsky

When I was a kid growing up on Long Island, there weren't many books in my house. There were a few magazines, most of which were next to the toilet, and occasionally, a copy of *Reader's Digest* would sneak its way in from somewhere out in the world. But I didn't get my hands on any of it, at least not as a kid. Whatever I knew about books in those days came from television.

Unfortunately, this meant that one of the earliest works of literature—and I use the term loosely—that I was exposed to was a book called *The Population Bomb*, written by a professor at Stanford University named Paul Ehrlich. According to this guy, who still works at Stanford and regularly hits the speaking circuit, there were way too many people on the earth in 1968, when he published the book. As the planet's population kept growing, food would get more and more scarce, and eventually—as in, a few years down the line—we would run out of food and mass starvation would ensue.

Here's a little taste, for anyone who hasn't read it:

"The battle to feed all of humanity is over....Hundreds of millions of people are going to starve to death....Nothing can prevent a substantial increase in the world death rate."

In the late 1970s when I was growing up, everyone believed that this was going to happen. We walked around with a constant fear that we were taking up too much space and that eventually, we were going to consume all the natural resources on the planet. When I got to college, I learned that this was a pretty popular opinion among university professors, especially ones who tended to lean left politically (as they almost all did, even in those days). Sitting in an economics class my sophomore year, I heard that soon we were going to run out of oil as well as food. According to my professor, the going rate for one barrel of this important natural resource would soon skyrocket, making it impossible to heat homes in the winter, cook food, or even get in our cars to escape. (As the owner of a sweet 1979 Camaro at the time, the last part was particularly devastating.)

But guess what?

It didn't happen. Nearly fifty years after Ehrlich first wrote *The Population Bomb*, not to mention a few hundred articles in the mainstream press that pushed the same doomsday message, we're all still here, and we're in better shape when it comes to the global food supply than we've ever been. The world, particularly the United States, also has more access to oil and gas than we ever have.

This has all been possible thanks to human ingenuity and innovation. We've got enough food because some of the best minds in science and agriculture invented new ways of growing food and manufacturing it. We've got access to energy because a group of Americans in the oil industry invented new and brilliant ways to extract oil from the ground. They invented horizontal drilling, which allows us to go under cities and natural rock formations to extract resources, and they invented fracking, which allows even more oil to come out of the ground (a process that is completely safe and environmentally friendly, despite what you might hear from the political left in this country).

The point?

We didn't run out of food. We didn't run out of oil and natural gas, either.

We didn't run out of these things because people with vision—vision rooted in an optimistic view of the world—invented new ways of doing things. Even when people told them that their work was hopeless and that no one would be able to stop the coming apocalypse, they persisted.

The same story has been playing itself out for centuries, and probably longer.

In England in the late eighteenth century, for instance, a Christian cleric named Thomas Robert Malthus grew quite famous for predicting the world was headed for doom. At the time, people in Britain were extremely worried about resources. People still grew most of the food they ate, and no one thought there was enough to go around. Writing in a book called *An Essay on the Principle of Population*, Malthus argued that poor people consumed too many resources, and that if the government continued to give these people aid, we would soon run out of food. He outlined something that became known as the "Malthusian Trap," which held that as long as the human population kept growing exponentially, farmers wouldn't have enough room to grow crops, and we would never have enough to feed the human population, which was growing exponentially at the time.

It's hard to stress how seriously people took this at the time. They took it so seriously, in fact, that Malthus was able to publish the same book eight times throughout the course of his life, changing the content only slightly by adding new facts and figures. Those around him truly believed that someday very soon, the food was going to run out, and the world was going to descend into a state of war.

Again, it didn't happen.

Today, the population of Britain is about eight times larger than it was when Malthus started writing, and the British agricultural industry supports them just fine (although the food, as anyone who's ever eaten in a British pub knows, still tastes a little like it was soaked in mop water, at least to those of us who grew up on Italian cuisine). The world has not fallen apart. The best among us—who, again, are the ones who choose to believe that the world is going to get better, not worse—have invented new ways of doing things, which have led to enormous amounts of prosperity and innovation.

Still, the pessimism persists. Today, if you crack open one of the many magazines written for liberal intellectuals, you'll still find pronouncements about how we're all headed for doom, and that we, the people, are the problem. Just a few years ago, the magazine *Scientific American* published a cover story called "Eight Billion People in the World Is a Crisis, Not an Achievement." The professor who wrote this article, like many new age intellectuals, has bought into the Malthusian line that people are a problem, and that having more of them is only going to create more problems.

If you speak to the average climate activist today, they'll tell you the same thing. Many nonprofits recommend strongly against having children. They'll say that the worst thing you can do for the environment—and, therefore, for your fellow men and women—is to multiply. Anyone who says otherwise, they'll claim, must not care about the climate.

At some point over the past few years, pessimism has become cool again. That's as true on Wall Street, where I spend most of my time during the week, as it is in the halls of science and government. For some reason, people will think you're smart and worldly when you tell them you think the whole world is going to hell. Complaining about the direction of the world and predicting that we're all headed for terrible things has become a way to signal to the crowd that you're enlightened. It means that you're "woke," to use the new phrase, and that you understand how terrible life has been for many people.

Optimism, on the other hand, can often get you laughed at. When you express a belief in the fundamental goodness of humankind or say something about how all people are basically nice when you approach them the right way, people start to think you're naive. They tell you that you're talking like some idiot politician running for president on a platform of unity and togetherness.

I've been hearing this my whole life.

Almost from the moment I was born, I've been surrounded by glass-half-empty kind of people. In my family, if you weren't predicting the worst, you weren't paying attention. To this day, I'm not sure why that was. Maybe it had something to do with "magical thinking." Members of my family seemed to believe that if you went around saying that the worst was going to happen, that was a way of making sure that the worst would never actually happen to you.

Of course, they had pretty good reasons to believe life was less than optimal. When she was still living in northeastern Pennsylvania, my grandmother had to bathe in a steel tub using hot water from a cistern. Even on Long Island, where we made our family home, my relatives often killed animals for dinner.

My point, I suppose, is that it's hard to be optimistic over the sound of screaming chickens.

Fortunately, optimism is a skill you can learn, just like anything else. No one is born being inherently optimistic. Even the guy at work who's happy all the time or your neighbor who never seems to complain about anything probably struggles with it from time to time. This is because there is no "optimism gene." There's nothing natural or unnatural about having an optimistic worldview. It is, rather, a mindset that one can choose to nurture every day.

The first step, of course, is to read what some of the smartest people in the world have said about optimism throughout history. Voltaire, the French Enlightenment writer, discusses the concept often in *Candide*, his satirical novella. In this book, Voltaire defines optimism as the belief that we live in the best of all possible worlds. Now, while this may appear naively idealistic, it offers a crucial insight. Optimism isn't about denying reality but rather choosing to focus on the positive aspects of it.

American psychologist Martin Seligman, known for his work on learned optimism, provides concrete strategies to nurture an optimistic mindset. Seligman suggests optimism is primarily a matter of explanatory style—the way we interpret and explain the events of our lives. If we learn to recognize and challenge our pessimistic self-talk, we can significantly foster a more optimistic worldview.

Seligman's ABCDE model outlines the process of cultivating optimism. "A" stands for adversity, the difficulties we encounter. "B" stands for beliefs, how we interpret adversity. "C" represents consequences, our feelings, and actions based on our beliefs. "D" symbolizes disputation, the process of challenging negative beliefs. Finally, "E" stands for energization, the positive feelings we experience when we successfully dispute our pessimistic beliefs.

Let's talk about something as simple as gratitude. Epictetus, the Stoic philosopher, maintained that we should not wish things to happen as we desire, but rather desire things to happen as they do. In essence, he was endorsing a practice of gratitude and acceptance.

You can cultivate gratitude by maintaining a daily gratitude journal. It's a straightforward routine where each day you write down three things you're thankful for. This simple exercise shifts your focus towards the positive aspects of your life, fostering an optimistic outlook.

Next, there's the power of perspective. The Greek tragedian Aeschylus once said, "Even in our sleep, pain which cannot forget falls drop by drop upon the heart until, in our despair, against our will, comes wisdom through the awful grace of God." Even in challenging situations, there's always a silver lining, a chance to learn and grow. Adopting a growth mindset, as propounded by psychologist Carol Dweck, allows us to view difficulties as opportunities, fostering an optimistic worldview.

Connecting with nature is another effective way to nourish optimism. Henry David Thoreau, the renowned naturalist, extolled the virtue of immersing oneself in nature, asserting that it brings us closer to our essence, inspiring tranquility and optimism. A regular walk in the park, tending to a garden, or simply observing the serenity of a sunset can do wonders for our mood and perspective.

Then there's the power of goal setting. The Greek philosopher Aristotle emphasized the concept of eudaimonia, the idea of flourishing or achieving one's full potential. By setting and working towards meaningful, achievable goals, we engage in a constructive pursuit that keeps us motivated, hopeful, and optimistic.

Moreover, surrounding yourself with optimistic people is beneficial. As social animals, we're influenced by those around us. By engaging with optimistic individuals, we're more likely to adopt a similar perspective.

Lastly, don't forget the importance of self-care. Ensuring a healthy diet, regular exercise, adequate sleep, and taking time out for relaxation and leisure activities are crucial for maintaining overall wellbeing, which, in turn, supports an optimistic outlook.

In the end, optimism is a symbol of leadership. No one wants to look to the front of an army and see a general who doesn't think he can win. Even if that general *doesn't* think he can win, he must put on a brave face and inspire his soldiers. The same goes if you're the head of a company or a teacher in a classroom. Like it or not, your words and actions—and even your nonverbal cues—set the tone for how everyone else is going to be feeling. If you walk in every day looking like the world is about to end, your employees are going to feel that way, too.

Also, pessimism is literally useless. It doesn't do anything for you. Anyone who's studied a little Buddhist philosophy knows how important it is to live in the moment, and not to anticipate bad things that haven't happened yet. As the old saying goes, why suffer in advance?

Sometimes, pessimism can make your situation worse. You can manifest defeat and choke in a pressure situation if you don't relax and believe.

Over the years, I've heard a few quotes on optimism that have spoken to me. Some come from ancient philosophers, while others come from the pages of books. One of my favorites is from the Israeli scientist Amos Tversky, who would later become famous for the groundbreaking work on cognitive psychology he did with Daniel Kahneman, author of *Thinking, Fast and Slow*. In the late 1960s, when Tversky was a student in the psychology department at the Hebrew University of Jerusalem, he used to tell people he was an optimist. In part, he said, this was simply due to his nature. But there were also practical reasons for it. He didn't see why anyone would live any other way.

"When you are a pessimist," he once said, "and the bad thing happens, you live it twice. Once when you worry about it, and the second time when it happens."

In other words, you get nothing from worrying. It only adds more pain to your life, and you get nothing in return.

When you learn to *stop* worrying, on the other hand, you'll realize you have a whole lot of time to spend on other things. You'll realize suddenly that you can see the best in every situation, and that you can see the best in people.

◌ Lesson 6

FIND MEANING

"He who has a why *to live for can
bear almost any* how."

—Friedrich Nietzsche

Once I got out of Port Washington and went to college, I started reading a lot. In the years since I first headed up to Boston to attend Tufts University, I've probably read a few thousand books. I've purchased about ten times that many.

If you don't believe me, check the background the next time you watch me do a television interview on Zoom. On the shelves behind me—not to mention the floor, the table, and the edges of my desk—you'll probably see big stacks of novels, business books, and long works of history that I've been working my way through. Right now, there's a copy of *Upgrade*, an excellent novel by Blake Crouch about the potential of science to turn human beings into cyborgs. I highly recommend it.

Elsewhere in my house, you'll find the books that have meant a great deal to me over the years. The classics I read in college cover about six hundred square feet of shelf space in my living room, for instance, as do books by friends of mine who've given them to me as gifts. I have biographies of just about every major president, and a complete collection of the works of Robert Greene, whose seven published books contain enough wisdom to last you ten lifetimes.

But there's one book that has meant more to me than any other. I've given copies of it out as gifts many times, and I reference it in casual conversation at least once a month.

Which is odd, considering the subject matter.

The book is *Man's Search for Meaning*.

Written over the course of about # years by a clinical psychologist named Viktor Frankl, the book tells the story of Dr. Frankl's experience in various Nazi concentration camps. He writes vividly about how he was taken from his home by the Nazis, along with thousands of other Jewish citizens of Germany at the time, and forced to do impossibly hard labor in several different concentration camps.

At the time Frankl arrived, very few people in the world knew about the horrors that the Nazis were perpetrating on the people of Europe. Many of the Jews Frankl traveled with believed they were being taken to the camps to work, and that they would be able to go home soon. They believed this, horrifically, because this is what they were told at the time they were taken. When they piled their belongings in buckets before being sorted into two groups—one group that would die, and another that would be forced to do hard labor until they also died—many of them thought they would soon get these items back.

As you'd expect from the short description above, Frankl's writing in *Man's Search for Meaning* can often be devastating. There are scenes that'll stick with you for years. Just reading about the people who marched into the gas chambers believing they were simply getting a shower before being shipped off to another camp is more than most people can take. Anyone who's ever worked hard on something will also flinch at the passage in which Frankl describes a concentration camp guard confiscating the manuscript of the book he was working on—what was, up until that point, his life's work—and throws it onto a pile of trash, where it'll stay until it gets burned with the bodies of the camp's prisoners.

As he worked in the concentration camp for months, fully believing that he was inching closer and closer to death every day, Frankl noticed some amazing things about human beings. One of the most amazing, looking back, is how comforting humor can be in dark times.

"Humor," he writes, "was another of the soul's weapons in the fight for self-preservation.

> "It is well known that humor, more than anything else in the human make-up, can afford an aloofness and an ability to rise above any situation, even if only for a few seconds. I practically trained a friend of mine who worked next to me on the building site to develop a sense of humor. I suggested to him that we would promise each other to invent at least one amusing story daily, about some incident that could happen one day after our liberation. He was a surgeon and had been an assistant on the staff of a large hospital. So I once tried to get him to smile by describing to him how he would be unable to lose the habits of camp life when he returned to his former work. On the building site (especially when the supervisor made his tour of inspection) the foreman encouraged us to work faster by shouting: "Action! Action!" I told my friend, "One day you will be back in the operating room, performing a

big abdominal operation. Suddenly an orderly will rush in announcing the arrival of the senior surgeon by shouting, 'Action! Action!'"

Reading about this experience, you're amazed at the ability of some people to keep a positive outlook on the world even during some of the darkest times human beings have ever experienced. It's hard to imagine anyone having it worse today than Frankl did in Europe in the early 1940s, but I'm sure you can imagine someone right now who's in a worse mood than he ever was over something that seems not to matter at all.

This is because Frankl, who was one of the top psychiatrists in Europe at the time he was taken by the Nazis, knew something that most of us don't. At least he thought about it more than almost anyone else. He knew that the true purpose of life on earth was not seeking out pleasure or acquiring as much stuff as possible. It wasn't about power, money, or even leaving behind a legacy.

The purpose of life on earth, according to Frankl, was meaning.

Even in the depths of despair, he and his fellow prisoners could pursue meaning every day, and it was this pursuit that would allow them to continue. Like most important things in life, this sounds almost stupid when you first read it. I mean, *of course* life is about finding meaning. What else would it be about?

But when you think a little more deeply about it, you'll realize that Frankl's insights were anything but obvious. At the time he was writing, two other psychologists—Sigmund Freud and Alfred Adler—had dominated the conversation about the purpose of human life. For Freud, it was pleasure, which he demonstrated in strange works such as *The Interpretation of Dreams*. For Adler, it was the connections we could forge with our fellow man. He believed that focusing on the people around you could erase your feelings of insecurity or inferiority.

Reading about this today, we can see the extent to which Frankl was right, while Freud and Adler were slightly off the mark. That's because his work, like all the best ideas in human history, have become so ingrained in our culture that we hardly even think about them anymore. The notion that we should live our lives in the pursuit of meaning and purpose is almost hardwired into us from an early age, so much so that reading a book about the subject seems unnecessary. It reminds me of a story about Winston Churchill, who, when he finished reading Aristotle's *Nicomachean Ethics*—one of the most important treatises on government and human nature ever written—closed the cover, turned to his friend, and said, "Well, it was good. But I knew all that already."

Some ideas, in other words, are so good, that they become part of the fabric of society. They work their way into the lessons we teach our kids, and they start showing up in the pages of self-help books. After a few decades, they become slogans stitched onto pillows and printed on the kind of posters you buy at Target. After *that*, they start showing up in books of wisdom written by hedge fund managers—which is when you know an idea has *really* arrived.

In general, this is a good process. The more people that have access to a good idea, the further that good idea can spread. But something also gets lost in the process. Some nuance goes away, and people start to take the wrong idea from the concept. For instance, when most people talk about "meaning" today, they tend to do it in terms that apply mostly to one, grand purpose. They speak about the meaning that comes from training to become a famous actor or a musician, as if everyone in the world needs to have one "dream" that they strive for.

But that's not the way the world works. Not everyone wants to play first base for the Yankees or become a Fortune 500 CEO. You don't need some grand ambition to find meaning. You don't even need to want to do anything more than what you're doing right now. If you love your job and want to keep doing it, you can still find meaning in life. If your greatest ambition is to get promoted to one level above where you are now, do that job for forty years, and retire, you can still find meaning.

This is because the way we tend to think about meaning—as a lifelong task that we must stick to forever—is not quite right. Rather than being objective and unchanging, meaning is made of small moments, and it's different for every person. The reason so many people are unsatisfied with their lives, according to Frankl, is that we think about meaning in the wrong way, as one thing that we should constantly strive for over the course of a lifetime rather than something that is constantly evolving based on our situation.

Toward the end of *Man's Search for Meaning*, Frankl tackles the inability of many people to see where true meaning lies.

In the beginning of this section, Frankl remembers his clinical practice—specifically a man who visited him and said, "I have nothing to expect from life anymore."

What sort of answer, Frankl wonders, can one give to that?

This is what he comes up with, which is better than anything I could have written. Apologies for the long quote, but I think you'll find it was worth it:

> What was really needed was a fundamental change in our attitude toward life. We had to learn ourselves and, furthermore, we had to teach the despairing men, that *it did not really matter what we expected from life, but rather what life expected from*

us. We needed to stop asking about the meaning of life, and instead to think of ourselves as those who were being questioned by life—daily and hourly. Our answer must consist, not in talk and meditation, but in right action and in right conduct. Life ultimately means taking the responsibility to find the right answer to its problems and to fulfill the tasks which it constantly sets for each individual.

These tasks, and therefore the meaning of life, differ from man to man, and from moment to moment. Thus, it is impossible to define the meaning of life in a general way. Questions about the meaning of life can never be answered by sweeping statements. "Life" does not mean something vague, but something very real and concrete, just as life's tasks are also very real and concrete. They form man's destiny, which is different and unique for each individual. No man and no destiny can be compared with any other man or any other destiny.

In other words, the job of pursuing meaning is one that you do every day. You'll often do it a few dozen times a day. Analyze the situation at hand, decide what life is asking from you, and then respond accordingly in the moment. Don't think about whether you're fulfilling some grand purpose or working toward a lofty goal. Just ask yourself if you're living up to your own principles, and whether you've responded the right way to that situation.

If you do that enough times, you'll find that your life is going in the right direction. Once you stop thinking about the grand narrative of your life and start doing the work—which can be extremely difficult sometimes—of responding to the "questions" that are being asked of you at every moment, you'll find that the larger story of your life becomes much better almost by accident.

"Don't aim at success," as Frankl puts it a little later in the book.

> The more you aim at it and make it a target, the more you are going to miss it. For success, like happiness, cannot be pursued; it must ensue, and it only does so as the unintended side effect of one's dedication to a cause greater than oneself or as the by-product of one's surrender to a person other than oneself. Happiness must happen, and the same holds for success: you have to let it happen by not caring about it. I want you to listen to what your conscience commands you to do and go on to carry it out to the best of your knowledge. Then you will live to see that in the long run—in the long-run, I say!—success will follow you precisely because you had *forgotten* to think about it.

By this point, you might as well just grab a copy of this guy's book and read it. I don't think I'm legally allowed to quote from it anymore without sending his publisher a big, fat check for copyright infringement.

When you do, you might find that the advice Frankl offers is a little less complicated than I'm making it seem here. You might find that the second half of the book, which describes his "logotherapy" in greater detail, is more helpful to you than the parts that spoke to me.

Or you might come away with exactly the same lessons that I've gotten from it over the years, specifically that it's meaning, not getting stuff or being praised for your work, that makes life worth living. And unlike the pursuit of money or houses or power, the pursuit of meaning can make you happy. It can bring you joy in a way that material things can't.

Most importantly, when you wake up every day and really ask what life is requiring of you—when you pursue meaning above all else—you'll find that happiness, as Frankl says, comes much more easily.

There's a story about Kurt Vonnegut that illustrates this point well. The modern philosopher Ryan Holiday tells it in his excellent book *Stillness Is the Key*. One summer, according to the story, Vonnegut was at a party in the Hamptons. If this party was anything like some of the summertime soirees I've been to in the area, I'm sure the backyard was all decked out. There were ice sculptures, champagne flutes, and enough trays of food to feed ten NFL football teams (who, of course, wouldn't have been allowed in).

Standing near the pool in his modest clothes, Vonnegut spotted his friend Joseph Heller, author of the book *Catch-22*. By this time, the book was already a smash hit. It had been on the bestseller list for decades, often right beside Vonnegut's book *Slaughterhouse-Five*. In terms of money, sales, and prestige, Vonnegut and Heller were pretty much as high up as it was possible for two writers to be. They were on top of the literary world.

Looking around at the opulent house, the yard, and the movie stars, Vonnegut turned to his friend and asked him, only half-jokingly, how it felt to know that this week alone, the guy who owned this house had made more money than *Catch-22* would ever make.

Heller thought for a moment, and said, "Fine. But I have something this guy will never have."

Vonnegut asked what it was.

"Enough," Heller said.

In other words, this guy—whose purpose in life was making up stories and writing them down—didn't care that he wasn't going to make as much money as a billionaire. His purpose in life gave him all the fulfilment he needed, and more money wasn't going to do anything for him. He knew what it was like to have enough, and he didn't waste his life pining for anything more.

This all comes back to joy, which we discussed in the very first lesson of this book. When you have joy, which often comes from knowing what your purpose is and waking up every day to work towards it, everything else stops mattering. The hits that will inevitably come your way stop hurting so much, and the world looks a little brighter. That doesn't mean you're not going to feel pain, because you absolutely will. But there is no pain that can't be overcome with a sense of purpose.

✎ Lesson 7

READ EVERYTHING

If you're holding this book, there's a good chance you're already a reader. At least I hope so. (I'd hate to think that this little tome is the only work of "literature" you're going to read this year.)

If that *is* the case, though, allow me to make the argument for reading more books—which, unfortunately, seems to be a lost art these days. And I really mean *reading*, by the way, not just scanning the reviews online or listening to podcasts with people who write the books.

Unless, of course, that podcast is *Open Book with Anthony Scaramucci*, in which case I thank you for your patronage.

Now, as you've probably noticed, I've got a lot of lessons kicking around in my head. Some of them come from real life. I screwed up, thought about what just happened, and derived some lessons from that process. But that can only get you so far.

When you're just starting out in life, one of the most important things you can do is gain an understanding of human nature—not just the good stuff, but the dark stuff, too. And since you probably don't want to spend too much of your time hanging out in court-rooms or prison cells (where the dark side of human nature is always on full display), the quickest way to gain this understanding is by reading books.

When I was a student at Tufts University outside of Boston, I knew I wanted to go into business eventually. So, most of my time was spent trying to make that happen. I read the *Wall Street Journal*, attended lectures by the CEOs of Fortune 500 companies, and took all the classes in accounting and finance that I could find in the course catalogue (which, in those days, was *literally* a catalogue, about the size of a phonebook).

That was all well and good.

But as the weeks of my freshman year wore on, I came to realize that there was something missing. I didn't feel like I was getting a full education by studying numbers and doing case studies about old companies. So, when it came time to sign up for spring classes, I decided to enroll in a few courses taught in the Department of Classical Studies. I had always loved to read, and I wanted to continue the habit in college. The problem was that it was often hard to tell which books were the best ones. I only had four years, after all.

I figured that the professors in the Classics Department would have some ideas about what was good. Time tends to be an impartial judge when it comes to books—and art and music, for that matter. Over time, the things that are unmemorable, overwritten, or just plain bad tend to fall away, leaving only the best. There's a reason we still study Homer, Ovid, Aristotle, and Shakespeare.

After thousands of years and hundreds of millions of readers—not to mention all the term papers and essays that have been written about them—these writers and thinkers are what's left. Their work has stood the test of time.

From the moment I cracked the cover on the first book I was assigned in the Classics Department, I was transfixed. Suddenly, I was sailing the "wine-dark sea" with Odysseus and his buddies. I was fighting in the Trojan War against Aeneas. For years, I'd been watching films and reading thriller novels that referenced these stories. Now, finally, I was seeing where it all came from.

Which, if you think about it, is what reading will do for you. It shows you where the stories you've been deeply familiar with for most of your life came from. Every year, thousands of college freshman crack the cover on *Hamlet* only to realize that it was the inspiration for *The Lion King*. Then, reading it and trying to figure out what William Shakespeare meant when he wrote all those dense, poetic lines, they discover that people have been wrestling for centuries with the same things we still think about today: identity, anxiety, and trying to find one's place in the world.

As we discussed a few pages ago, there are several narratives that come up again and again in literature. We have the hero's journey, the tragedy, and the Shakespearean comedy, all repeated throughout the years by people who feel that they can take these forms and do something new and interesting with them. This repetition doesn't happen because people are lazy and can't come up with plots of their own. It happens because human beings have realized over the course of the six thousand years in which we've been telling one another stories and writing them down that there is something in these forms that speaks to what it means to be a human being.

If you check the shelves of your local bookstore right now, you'll find variations on several themes that were set out by our ancient predecessors. As of this writing, the crime writer Don Winslow is publishing a series of crime novels about life in Providence, Rhode Island, the first two of which are called *City on Fire* and *City of Dreams*. Most people who pick up copies at the airport will read these books and find characters who come alive on the page, a plot that thrills them, and more witty lines than you can get in most stand-up comedy specials.

But readers who've studied the whole of the Western canon will see something much richer and deeper in the story. They'll see that Winslow based the whole trilogy on *The Aeneid*, one of the oldest and most cherished epic poems in world literature. In that story, first told by the Roman poet Virgil, is Aeneas, a soldier fighting in the Trojan War. Instead of finding his way home, he escapes Troy and finds that the world has changed around him. And he becomes his own hero.

The same thing is true of films you see. Take the film *Jurassic Park*, which came out thirty years ago this year, as an example. At the time of its release, the film was a monster. It was further proof that Steven Spielberg would be one of the most important directors of his time, and it also introduced the world (although most people didn't know it) to a young screenwriter named David Koepp, who'd go on to write many more excellent films and novels over the course of his career.

On its face, the film was a simple disaster flick about a park full of dinosaurs that descends into disaster. The T. rex gets hungry for blood, and it eats a guy while he's on the toilet; velociraptors chase kids through the theme park until they mount a daring escape by helicopter as the dinosaurs fight it out in grand fashion. It was a thrill ride, which is why it made $47 million on the weekend it opened.

Now, you can watch that movie for the action and have a good time. You can probably watch it again and have just as much fun as you did the first time. But when you start to recognize that the storyline of the film is about much more than just dinosaurs coming to life—that there's chaos theory, a critique of capitalism, and several other ancient storylines built into it—you get to see it differently, and (I think) to enjoy it more deeply.

You might not know, for instance, that *Jurassic Park* is based on a novel by Michael Crichton, who saw the book as his chance to pay homage to the book *Frankenstein*. Both books, as Crichton saw it, deal with men who are obsessed with creating monsters. They do so with a sense that they are more powerful than God, and that hubris comes back to bite them in the ass.

From there, you might be interested to know that even *Frankenstein*, which was written by Mary Shelley—who, amazingly, was only nineteen at the time—in 1816, is based on the even older tale of Prometheus, a figure in Greek mythology who famously tried (and was caught) stealing fire from the gods. In that story, Prometheus, who was the son of Titan Iapetus, attempts to bring fire down from heaven to give human beings the same power of imagination and creation that the gods have. When he's caught, the gods punish him by chaining him to a rock and having a raven peck out his liver, over and over again, for eternity.

By this point, you might be wondering: *Who gives a shit?*

Well, I do. And you should, too, even if you weren't a classics major or a big reader in your younger years. You should give a shit because filling up your mind with the best thoughts that other human beings have to offer—which they wrote down, quite conveniently, in books—is just as important to your mental health as lifting weights and eating right can be to your physical health. If you want to play any major role in human events, even a small one, it's incumbent upon you to read the stories of the men and women who've tried to do so before you.

You can start anywhere. Pick up something that was published yesterday, or Google a list of "100 great books to read before you die." Better yet, flip to the back of this book and choose something from my own list of great books to read before you die. (I figured it'd be kind of a dick move to go on for a dozen pages or so about the importance of reading without telling you *what* I think you should read.)

When you start reading books—whether it's the ones I've suggested or the ones you're finding on your own—and really paying attention to what's inside them, you'll notice (happily, I hope) that there are almost no original stories in the world. Everything is based on something else. Even the book you're holding is the product of many hundreds of books, conversations, and other interactions that I've had over the course of my life. Almost nothing I'm saying is original, even the things that relate to my own experience. It all comes from other people whom I've had the good sense to listen to and read over the years.

I hope that's comforting to you because it is to me.

Every time I've read a book or had a conversation with someone who's smarter than I am—which, for a while, was just about everyone I met—I filed away another piece of information, or another story that could help me understand the world and the mystery of my own existence. The writing of people who've been dead for a long time is, among other things, confirmation that the questions we struggle with today aren't new ones. Writers and thinkers have been wondering whether God exists for centuries; they've been wondering why we're here on earth in the first place for even longer than that.

Bringing this kind of thing up at the dinner table or over drinks with friends—although fine in moderation—can make you seem like kind of a psycho. But contemplating these questions is, at least in my opinion, one of the most important things that human beings can do with our time on earth. It can provide a sense of meaning that is often missing in today's world, when we feel that all the information we need is out there on the internet (although you'll notice that almost no one ever goes out looking for it).

I'm sure you've seen that today lots of people know a lot about very specific things. Musicians know a lot about music, writers know a lot about books, and people know a whole lot about their own politics. Primarily, this is thanks to cable news, social media, and other forces that have split us up into different echo chambers. I'm willing to bet that there's not a viewer of Fox News in the country who can't tell you the finer points of the Hunter Biden laptop scandal, just like everyone who watches MSNBC can tell you that the Trump campaign "colluded with Russia."

The sad thing? Both groups sincerely believe that the *other* group is insane.

When we only listen to what we want to hear—and when we only get our information from television and the internet—we get a very skewed sense of reality. We get news that confirms the beliefs we had when we turned on the television, and we get videos that are tailored to a specific algorithm. There's almost nowhere we can go to contemplate the things that bring us together rather than drive us apart.

But books are a good place to go when you want to be reminded of the shared inheritance of all human beings. Reading through some of the best works of literature, you'll find quotes that everyone knows. By reading the stories that surround those quotes, you'll realize *why* everyone knows them. You also might begin to understand history and politics a little better.

There was a time, for instance, when politicians who gave speeches could assume everyone they were speaking to shared a common set of references. Presidents often quoted obscure parts of the Bible and lines from Shakespeare, knowing everyone in the audience would be on board. Politicians could assume this as late as the early 1900s because we used to require that kids read classic literature in school, especially at the level of the university. Today, we don't think that's quite as important, and our politics has suffered for it.

Compare the last speech you heard a president or a senator give with this, which comes from President Abraham Lincoln's second inaugural address:

> With malice toward none, with charity for all, with firmness in the right as God gives us to see the right, let us strive on to finish the work we are in, to bind up the nation's wounds, to care for him who shall have borne the battle and for his widow and his orphan, to do all which may achieve and cherish a just and lasting peace among ourselves and with all nations.

On the cold, rainy afternoon when Lincoln first spoke those words, the nation was more divided than it had ever been. The Civil War, which had already killed more than six hundred thousand Americans, was still raging, although the Union was on its way to victory. But no one knew what would become of the people who'd been at one another's throats for so long, or how many more people were going to have to die before the war officially ended.

When Lincoln spoke, he reached for references that everyone in the crowd—whether Black or white, southern or northern—could understand. He attempted to use a common set of references that would make people understand one another. And he was able to do that because the people who gathered to listen to him that day had all read the same Bible, grown up with the same stories, and studied the same ancient myths. When Lincoln made references to the Bible—which abounded in his second inaugural—everyone was on the same page, so to speak. When he talked about old stories that everyone had learned in school, he was speaking to people in a common language, attempting to remind everyone in the crowd that not a single one of them was morally superior to the other; they were all children of God.

I think we could use a little more of that.

Don't you?

So, go read some of the best stuff we have to offer, and see if you can remember most of what you read. That, as the third-grade teacher who made you memorize the Gettysburg Address can tell you, is when you get true understanding.

Speaking of which...

In the end, we all live inside our heads. And if you believe Elon Musk, we could all be living in a simulation, meaning that the stuff in your head is actually the only real thing in the world. (Of course, that's the kind of thing that makes my head hurt, so let's not dwell on it too much.)

But the point still stands. As we discussed earlier, your entire experience of the world happens right between your ears. Everything is in your mind, whether you like it or not. So, you might as well furnish the room of your mind with the best stuff around. That means picking books at random just to see what's inside. It means revisiting classic works of literature—the things that have stood the test of time, moving through the best minds in world history—and seeing what else you can get from them. Don't be afraid to pick up something that might not interest you. You'll often find that in the hands of a good writer, any story can be good.

So, my advice? Pick up a book and start reading. It doesn't matter what it is. Give it about thirty pages or so, and if you *really* hate it—as in, you hate the characters, or the writing is so rough that turning another page seems impossible—go try something else. But keep the first one on your shelf, because you never know when you might return to it and find something in it that speaks to you in a way you couldn't have imagined before.

It's happened to me. I remember reading some books for the first time and thinking it was nonsensical. I couldn't make heads or tails of the plot or what anyone was saying. Then, just a few years ago, I picked it back up again and the whole thing sang. I got it.

After a while, you'll be surprised at how often you find yourself revisiting the things you've read. Oddly enough, it often happens during the hardest times of your life. I can't tell you how many times I thought about passages from the work of Viktor Frankl, whose work was discussed in the last lesson. Waking up in the months after I was fired from the White House, I would often take out a book and read, happy that the sun had come up that day, and that I was still lucky enough to live in the same house as my wife and kids.

Even when I didn't have access to books, I'd think back on some of the best lines of poetry and prose in my head—both things that I had memorized purposefully, and things that lodged themselves in my head without my even realizing it.

Again, your mind is like a room. The way you decorate that room is up to you. Either you can scroll endlessly through your phone, filling the room of your mind with TikTok jokes and hate-filled headlines from your Apple News app, or you can kick back with the works of Aristotle, Leo Tolstoy, or masterful modern authors like Daniel Silva. You can even find a dusty book of poetry in a used bookstore and read the first poem in the collection over and over again, repeating the words until you start to figure out what they mean.

The great thing about all of this, of course, is that once a few lines like that are in your head, they stay there more or less forever. You can pull it out whenever you need, repeating the same lines, deriving endless pleasure from the experience.

The reading mind grows and remains forever excited and curious.

Every few years, we see an article in the *New York Times* or some other news outlet that says book sales are declining. I remember about two decades ago, just as I was kicking around ideas for what would become my first book, *Goodbye, Gordon Gekko*, there were news stories written every day about how e-readers were going to kill physical books because they were cheaper, easier to get, and more convenient to read than big twenty-eight-dollar hardcovers.

For a while, that seemed to be true. We saw a decline in physical book sales, and we lost a few great local bookstores. After that, we lost some great chains, such as Borders and B. Dalton. It made sense in the grand scheme of things, given how many print newspapers were going bust every day with the advent of sites like Craigslist and social media.

But something changed.

As time went on, people seemed to realize that it was pleasant carrying around a nice thick book and taking it out when you got a few spare moments. You could take these to the beach, read them outside in the full glare of the sun, and they still worked after you dropped them in the pool (provided you left them out to dry for a few hours in the right conditions).

If you look through history, some of the top minds in business have always bet on books. Think about it. When Jeff Bezos got the idea for the company that would become Amazon in the early 1990s, he didn't have much to go on. What he knew, according to a recent interview, was that the number of internet users in the world was growing at about 2,300 percent every year, and that anything that was growing at that rate—even if it was only baseline, at-home use—was going to become huge. So, he decided to open an online marketplace.

As Bezos tells the story today, he made dozens of lists of products he could sell. He thought about creating a shoe store, a record store, and an online electronics shop. The possibilities were endless. In the end, he settled on books. He did so, he says, because books are roughly the same size and weight. As he put it, "There are more items in the book category than there are items in any other category by far."

Since then, Amazon has become the largest and most efficient marketplace in the history of the world. They still sell books in astounding quantities. In fact, when traditional bookstores are deciding which titles to order, they look to see who's pre-ordered the book on Amazon. The more people who've done that, the more copies they'll order for the shelves.

If you follow me on Twitter, you probably know I'm a big fan of new technologies. If you don't know, go check out the book I wrote about how Bitcoin is going to save the world. (Which is called *The Sweet Life with Bitcoin*, and available, oddly enough, only on Amazon).

But I also respect durable technologies that don't need much in the way of updates. And that's exactly what books are. As Bezos has said, the book is arguably the most durable technology. It has arguably had a "year one" that's lasted 500 years.

So, if you want to be a productive member of society, go get some and start reading.

I promise, it'll change your life.

❧ Lesson 8

DISCIPLINE YOURSELF BECAUSE NO ONE ELSE IS GOING TO DO IT

You found your purpose?

Great. That was the hard part.

Now comes the easy part.

You've had your moment of inspiration. You've sat down with your journal or did a quick meditation session, and you've realized what you'd like to do with your life. You know where you want to be.

The rest is just hard work.

When I say hard work, of course, you probably think I'm talking about waking up at four o'clock in the morning, Mark Wahlberg style, and hitting the gym three times before going to the office. Maybe in your case I am.

But for most people, establishing a routine that challenges you and sticking to it will be more than enough. Then, over time, as your mind and body get stronger, you'll have more control over yourself, and you'll be able to achieve a little more every day.

Sadly, most people don't learn how to do this in school. They believe the people who have control over their own minds and bodies are simply born tougher than everyone else. This is largely because when we go to school every day, we have people who handle the discipline for us. We get held in for recess when we don't do our homework, and we get sent out of the room for acting up in class. I know it happened to me several times over the course of my not-so-illustrious junior high school career.

Then, suddenly, there is no one holding us accountable. Sure, we have college professors and then bosses who'll fail us or write us up for failing to do the right thing, but that's only in one small segment of our lives. Even the laziest people in the world can avoid getting in trouble at work. The trouble comes when we get home from work and have to turn our attention to the project that really excites us—the YouTube channel, the side hustle, or the Great American Novel sitting in a folder on our laptops.

These are the things that no one is waiting for, and that's what makes them so hard to finish. There's no editor calling every few minutes demanding the first draft of your novel, and there are no board members looking over your shoulder to make sure you set up your business in a timely and efficient manner. The only person who can make you get out of bed and work toward your purpose is you.

I'm sure that if you're like most people—and even if you're more motivated than the average person—you won't feel like doing that every day. You'll want to hit the snooze button in the morning, scroll through Instagram on your lunchbreak, and go to bed early rather than staying up to get the extra work done. This is when you'll start to negotiate with yourself. You'll say that you worked hard at your day job all day, and you're too tired to keep plugging away at your passion project.

I probably don't have to tell you that this negotiating with yourself is bad. When you listen to the little voice in your head that tells you not to work too hard—whether it's working out or sitting down at your desk to crank away at a project—you're failing to live up to your potential. That might feel good in the short term, but in the long term, it's going to make you feel empty. Think about it. I'm sure you can recall a day recently when instead of getting up and getting to work you sat around and did nothing. Maybe you chilled out on the couch on a day you were supposed to be working from home, moving your mouse around and sending a few nonsense emails so your colleagues thought you were working.

How did you feel at the end of that day? Did all the scrolling through social media feeds and laying on the couch make you feel as good as you thought it would?

I'm willing to bet that it didn't.

Now, picture the opposite. Try to remember a day when you got up and did something you really didn't want to do. Maybe it was a time when you got up and hit the gym to train for a big race, or when you powered through all the complex, annoying tasks that had been sitting in your inbox for weeks. While that was happening, I'm sure you felt a great deal of strain. I'm sure there were brief seconds when you wanted to quit. But when the day was over, you got to sit down and enjoy yourself—to feel true, unadulterated joy—because you had clocked another day of working toward your purpose.

I'm not saying you must love getting up and getting shit done. No one loves that. But I *am* saying you must learn to love effort—

the feeling that you're working toward something that you are not certain you'll be able to accomplish—and get used to being uncomfortable. When you start to *like* the feeling of being in an uncomfortable place, you'll grow. You'll find that you can do more today than you could do yesterday, and your outlook on the world is more positive than it was before. This is because you'll be growing and getting better every day, which makes you feel good.

If you don't believe me, consider the life story of one of our greatest presidents.

When most people picture Teddy Roosevelt, their first thoughts are probably of a tough guy on a horse, riding over the plains and commanding armies during the Spanish-American War. They picture his broad shoulders, his thick moustache, and an unmistakable charisma that made him one of the most beloved presidents in this country's history.

Maybe some people think he just showed up that way, coming out of his mother's womb with that big moustache and tough-guy attitude intact.

But he didn't.

In fact, when Roosevelt was a young boy, he had asthma so bad that he couldn't even handle having someone scold him without devolving into coughing fits and panic attacks. His body was misshapen and small, and he had trouble participating in even the most basic sports. While the other kids were out playing around his house, young Roosevelt was inside, often being carried through the halls of the second floor by his father to stop the coughing fits that kept him up at night.

For some people, being born with this kind of illness would have been a license to lounge around forever. Many of us wouldn't have been able to break out of the cycle of helplessness that Roosevelt was born into. We would have gotten used to staying in bed most of the day, reading the paper, and having our meals brought to us by servants while we wallowed in our own misery.

This would have been especially easy for Roosevelt given that he had the good fortune to have been born into a wealthy and respected family. He'd also been born with the gift of a first-rate mind. As a young man, Roosevelt read constantly. He also kept voluminous notebooks, in which he recorded his thoughts about what he was reading, what he was doing, and everything he was seeing in nature. By the time he was old enough to walk through the woods surrounding his childhood home, he'd already recorded notes about nearly every species of bird and animal that lived there. This was the kind of life he could have maintained quite happily, even with a broken body.

But he wanted more. And thankfully, his father told him how to get it.

"Theodore," his father wrote in a letter when he was twelve years old, "you have the mind but you have not the body, and without the help of the body the mind cannot go as far as it should. You must *make* your body. It is hard drudgery to make one's body, but I know you will do it."

In other words, the only way out of this horrible condition was by force. Rather than wandering the woods aimlessly and hoping that his body would fix itself, Roosevelt would have to hit the gym and build himself up slowly.

In practice, this was brutal. At the time he started making daily visits to a gymnasium in town, the twelve-year-old Roosevelt was tall, skinny, and tired all the time. His chest cavity was shrunken. And, as his biographer Edmund Morris writes, "The lungs crammed into that narrow cavity were themselves crammed with asthma, and the mere act of breathing placed a strain on his heart."

But he hit the weights anyway, swinging kettlebells and lifting barbells, often going until he collapsed onto the floor.

At first, it was drudgery, just like his father told him it would be. I'm sure anyone who has gone to the gym for a few days in a row can understand just how disheartening it is to lift weights, get sore, and find yourself so tired the next day that you never want to go back. And most of us weren't born with asthma, brittle bones, and a body that always seems on the verge of falling apart.

But the young Roosevelt believed he had no other choice. Over the course of days and weeks that eventually became months and years, he kept up his workout routine, doing a few more reps each time and finally finding that he could increase the weight as well. Over time, he took up running and swimming, amazing himself with how quickly his muscles seemed to be growing. His mental well-being increased, too. According to Morris's biography, the summer he began his workout routine was the first time in his life that the young Roosevelt went more than a few weeks without mentioning his illness in his diary.

That's not to say there weren't bumps in the road. About two years after he started his workout routine, for instance, the young Roosevelt took a trip up to Moosehead Lake, believing the fresh air would be good for his asthma. On the stagecoach ride there, he came across a group of kids who seemed intent on messing with him.

About these kids, Roosevelt wrote in his diary, "They found that I was a foreordained and predestined victim, and industriously proceeded to make life miserable for me. The worst feature was that when I finally tried to fight them, I discovered that either one singly could not only handle me with easy contempt, but handle me so as not to hurt me much and yet prevent my doing any damage whatever in return."

In other words, he got his ass kicked.

Big time.

Before that ride, I'm sure Roosevelt was feeling like he could take on the world. His chest had grown considerably from where it had been a few months earlier, and his arms were pumped up from the weights he'd been lifting. He knew because he recorded the exact measurements every day in his diary.

But it didn't matter. To the kids on the stagecoach, whose bodies had been normal sized their whole lives, young Teddy was still a little shrimp. They were bigger, and they'd had more advantages in life, and so they decided to pick on someone smaller than they were to make themselves feel better. It's a tale as old as time.

Getting off the stagecoach at Moosehead Lake, I'm sure Roosevelt felt like giving up. Getting beaten up by a group of kids who are bigger than you, as I found out repeatedly growing up in Port Washington, can really take the fight out of a guy. It can make you feel like whatever you've been doing up to that point hasn't been good enough, if only because it ended with you getting beaten down by people bigger than you.

But again, Teddy Roosevelt kept going. Rather than retreating into his bedroom with his books and journals, he decided to spend twice as much time in the gym as he'd been spending for the past two years. He also signed up for boxing lessons.

Every day for the rest of his life, Roosevelt worked out his body and his mind. He kept up the routine that he started when he was twelve years old, and the results were amazing. During his lifetime, among other things, he was a New York City police commissioner, warrior, vice president, and president.

At first glance, it might seem like I've included this anecdote here to convince you that hitting the gym is going to make you successful. Maybe that's true. But it's not why I think the story of Teddy Roosevelt's early life is so amazing.

It's amazing because it's the story of someone who showed up every day no matter how he was feeling, dragged himself through a routine, and achieved great things because of his willingness to keep going. I'm sure most of the days he showed up to work out, especially when he was first getting started, were extremely painful. I would imagine that even when he was a big, broad-shouldered general who could lift more weight than most professional bodybuilders of the time, there were days when he didn't want to work out or do any physical exercise. But he did it anyway.

The reason he did it anyway is not because he wanted to achieve the perfect body to impress people. He knew as well as anyone that there's really no such thing as the perfect body. No matter how much you work out, you're not going to wake up one day and be satisfied. That's the wrong way to think about work. What Teddy Roosevelt knew—and what so many great leaders know—is that if you show up every day and attack your work with intensity, doing it even when you would rather blow your brains out, you start to fall in love with the process itself.

And *that*—loving the work rather than the reward—is what will allow you to find true joy in life.

⚹ Lesson 9

TAKE RISKS

*"Progress always involves risk. You can't steal
second base and keep your foot on first."*

—Frederick B. Wilcox

When I was twenty-seven years old, I had a pretty good gig, especially when you consider where I came from. Every day, I boarded a train from Tarrytown and headed to the Goldman Sachs building at 85 Broad Street. I finally had enough money to wear clothes that didn't make me look like an extra in a John Travolta movie, and I was doing pretty well for myself in the office. In the span of a few years, I had paid off my student debt and purchased a small house.

Walking out the door every evening, sometimes well past nine or ten o'clock, I got the sense that I could stay at Goldman Sachs and climb the ladder all the way to the top. There were certainly precedents for that. I saw them every day.

Robert Castrignano, one of the people who mentored me from the second I walked in the door, had climbed that very ladder, and he looked happy from where I was sitting. So did all the guys who worked in big offices on the floors above mine, wearing custom suits and deciding which of their four houses their family was going to lounge around in that summer.

Beyond the opulence and the money, a career at Goldman Sachs came with security. That would have been tempting for anyone in the late 1980s, when I really started to settle in at the firm, but it was especially important for me. As a kid, I had been devastated to see my father get his hours cut, and I didn't want the same thing to happen to me. Although there was a lot that could go wrong if I decided to stay at Goldman Sachs—I could be shown the door after a few nice trades, for instance—I could be relatively certain that as long as I kept performing well, maintaining good relationships, and not screwing up, I could climb the ladder and end up near the top of the organization by the time I was in my late middle age.

Several times, the people who worked above me said so explicitly. If I kept my head down, they said, I would do very well here. I would be able to have a life that most people in the United States can only dream about.

But something was nagging at me. I didn't quite know how to describe it at the time, but now I recognize it as the feeling that I wasn't fulfilling my purpose in life. I know, I know, that sounds like I'm sitting on the couch of the Oprah Winfrey show circa 2004 or so, but it's true. I knew that the reason I was on earth was to run my own business, and there was no amount of money—even if that money came in the form of enormous bonus checks from a major organization like Goldman Sachs—that was going to make me feel better about not doing that. There was a hole inside me, and it was getting bigger every day that I clocked into the office and worked for someone else.

So, I quit.

Today, when people ask me why I left a job like that—usually when they're thinking about doing something similar in their own lives—I'll respond with a joke. I tell them that I quit "because I was an idiot."

And it's true. By any objective measure, leaving the job that I had at the age I left it was a stupid thing to do. Nine times out of ten, I would have ended up back in the lobby of my old building begging for a job scrubbing toilets, having lost all the money I took to start the new business and fallen flat on my face.

But somehow, largely thanks to luck and a crazy work ethic, that didn't happen. I founded my first company, Oscar Capital, shortly after leaving Goldman Sachs. A few years after that, in 2001, I sold Oscar Capital to Neuberger Berman.

That seemed like a victory at the time. I got a great paycheck. My employees were taken care of. Most importantly, I was validated. The risk I had taken when I left Goldman Sachs for the first time had paid off, and my identity as an entrepreneur was solid. Finally, after years of working for other people, I had managed to build something which, by any objective standard, was good. It had sold, after all.

There was one problem. The company we'd sold to, Neuberger Berman, merged with Lehman Brothers in 2001, which effectively made me an employee all over again. To make matters worse, I wasn't getting paid as much as I thought I should be, and my personality didn't quite line up with the personalities of those around me. I know this because every year the firm made us all take Myers-Briggs personality tests to make sure we could work together effectively.

I didn't do so well on mine. I can remember the Lehman personnel director telling me, "You know, Anthony, very few people here at Lehman had your results."

So, I had a choice (kind of). Either I could try to shape up and change my personality, trying hard to impress my new overlords so they'd give me more money and more responsibility. Silly as that option might sound now, it seemed viable at the time. As you might know, I can bullshit with the best of them. If I really put my mind to it, I'm sure I could have convinced these people that I had enough Lehman team spirit to make my way toward upper management.

But that would have been lying. And as we'll see in a few pages, lying is one of the worst things you can do for your soul.

So, I decided that I was going to quit again.

For some reason, even though the second company clearly was not a good fit for me, I felt more fear and trepidation turning in my papers than I had when I'd left Goldman Sachs. I think it had something to do with the risk. Everyone, I assumed, could pull off an unlikely victory one time, especially with the arrogance of youth on their side. When I left Goldman Sachs, I didn't really know how hard it would be to start my own business, so I went into the task with everything I had. I didn't know whether I would be able to do it twice.

There was a moment there—which, admittedly, didn't last very long—when I wondered if sticking around being someone's employee might be the safe thing to do for a while. It would certainly allow me to relax a little, and not to worry so much about whether my income is going to disappear in a matter of hours (which is always a risk when you decide to start your own business).

But I left anyway.

Something in me knew that if I stayed, things weren't going to work out. Which, admittedly, wasn't all that hard to notice, given that I'd been told several times I wasn't a good fit. But rather than trying to fit in, I quit yet another job to start another business.

A few years later, Lehman Brothers—my safe option—collapsed in spectacular fashion. All the people I had once worked with lost their jobs in a matter of minutes, as did the people who administered my personality tests from a few floors above me. The bankruptcy of Lehman Brothers sent shockwaves through the financial world.

Don't get me wrong; I wasn't immune either. Having started SkyBridge Capital in 2005, I was in full-on panic mode, and so were my new partners. But together, we charted our own course and a way out of the crisis.

Most importantly, we started the SALT conference, which is still going to this day (and more popular than ever). Even that, as you read in the prologue to this book, was a huge risk. All my partners advised against it. But something in my gut told me it was the right move, and thankfully, I was right.

Sometimes, trusting your gut works out. But that requires paying close attention to what's going on inside your head, too—knowing what life is asking from you at every moment, just like Viktor Frankl said—and making your decisions based on meaning. Is the risk you're about to take going to bring you closer to fulfilling your purpose in life?

If so, go ahead and do it.

The comedic actor Jim Carrey, famous for roles in *Dumb and Dumber* and *The Mask*, has a great story about this. As a kid, he wanted to be an actor more than anything, but he was often led to believe that a life in the arts wasn't stable. You could never know when your next paycheck was coming in, and that's *if* you managed to get the first one, which is never guaranteed in Hollywood. For a while, he considered following the path that had been set out by his father, who had given up his aspirations to become a jazz musician and taken a safe job as an accountant.

Then, one day, something happened that changed his life forever.

"When I was twelve years old," he says, "[my father] was let go from that safe job. Our family had to do whatever we could to survive. I learned many great lessons from my father, not the least of which is that you can fail at what you don't want, so you might as well take a chance on doing what you love."

As you can see, even safety isn't always safe.

You never know.

Now, does that mean you should quit your job and start auditioning to be in comedies, hoping you'll become the next Jim Carrey? Not necessarily. What you're meant to do—what the universe is asking from you—will be different from what it's asking from everyone else. The main goal of your life, as we've talked about already, is to identify what that is.

Then, once you do, don't be afraid to scrap all potential backup plans—especially the ones that feel like the "safe," boring option. Eventually, I think you'll find that even if you don't get fired from that job the way Jim Carrey's father did, knowing that you didn't take a chance on yourself is going to eat at you. You'll become toxic to those around you, and you'll wish you had taken the chance when you knew it was right.

The operative phrase here, of course, is "knew it was right." Although you can never really know when it's the right time to take a big risk, you can feel it. You can.

My friend Matt Higgins, an entrepreneur and television star who scraped his way to the top after dropping out of high school, has a great book about this. The title, *Burn the Boats*, refers to an old strategy that military leaders have been using for centuries to ensure victory.

In short, this strategy is about cutting off all options but one, "burning the boats" so you have nothing to do but charge ahead. Either you succeed, or you die (metaphorically speaking). Having a plan B, he writes, "weakens our resolve and diminishes our chances for breakout success."

Early in the book, he quotes Ralph Waldo Emerson, who wrote in his famous essay "Self-Reliance" that we all must "learn to detect and watch that gleam of light which flashes across [our minds] from within, more than the lustre of the firmament of bards and sages."

In other words, when you're assessing whether to take a risk, look inward. Don't worry about the external metrics, and don't worry what you're going to do if you fail.

Maybe you're contemplating taking a big risk right now, and you want some advice on whether it's the right thing to do. Maybe you're looking to make a pro/con list or a chart that'll tell you whether you've got the right idea.

But there is no chart, and pro/con lists can only get you so far.

Look inward. You already know whether this is the right move.

ஜ Lesson 10

GIVE MORE
THAN YOU GET

*"Life's persistent and most urgent question
is, 'What are you doing for others?'"*

—Martin Luther King, Jr.

When I say "giving," especially in the context of a book that's largely about business, you probably think I'm talking about charitable giving. You probably think I'm about to tell you that life becomes much more meaningful when you take a great deal of the money you have and give it away to worthy causes—when you donate to foundations, attend charity dinners, and try to get all your friends to give money to those same causes.

Well, it's true.

Throughout my career, I've given a lot of money away. Some of it has gone to political candidates, which has been effectively useless. (Notably, I cut a big check to Barack Obama, who was a former colleague of mine at Harvard Law School, only to have the guy turn around and tell me what shitheads me and my Wall Street buddies were.)

But the most rewarded I've ever felt in my life, outside of things involving my family, have involved charitable giving. I know many people (whose names you probably know, too) who feel the same way.

One of them is Joe Torre, who managed the New York Yankees during a great period in the team's history. Of course, it wasn't so great for me, a Met fan, but I can appreciate greatness when I see it.

But under all that success, there is a dark story that few people know about. Only the most dedicated biographers of Joe Torre—who made a point to dig into the gloomiest corners of the man's life—found out about it. Born on July 18, 1940, in Brooklyn, New York, Joe Torre was bred in the crucible of a household overshadowed by domestic violence. Joe's father was a New York City police officer who held a heavy hand, often leading to severe physical confrontations with Joe's mother, Margaret. Young Torre grew up against this backdrop of aggression and fear, his childhood marred by the wounds of this familial conflict.

That kind of experience sticks with you, which is why even at the height of his success, Joe Torre couldn't shake what happened to him during his childhood. He wanted to make sure that no child would ever have to endure domestic violence the way he did—at least not without having a place to go to feel safe.

In 2002, he founded the Joe Torre Safe at Home Foundation alongside his wife, Ali. The foundation was established with a vision to educate and end the cycle of domestic violence. The heart of the organization's mission was to provide children with a voice, a means to speak up and share their experiences with violence and find healing in the process.

One of the foundation's most impactful initiatives is Margaret's Place, named in honor of Torre's mother. These safe rooms, installed in schools across the nation, offer kids a secure environment where they can discuss their experiences and feelings with professional counselors, and learn to cope with their circumstances.

Today, the Safe at Home Foundation stands as a beacon of hope for countless children and families. It's a testament to Torre's belief in the power of giving back, a belief that he cultivated from his childhood and carried with him into his illustrious career and beyond. It's a legacy that extends beyond the baseball diamond, reaching into the heart of society, transforming lives, one safe space at a time.

In the end, Joe Torre's story is more than a tale of a boy from Brooklyn who became a baseball legend. It's a story of a man who understood that the essence of life isn't just in achieving greatness but in using that greatness to spark change. It's about recognizing that the key to happiness and fulfillment lies not just in what we attain for ourselves, but in what we are able to give.

In the years since Torre started Safe at Home, I've been incredibly proud to contribute to his organization. I know better than most people how dark things can get for kids who feel like they're not safe in their own homes. Safe at Home has done amazing things, and I look forward to the work ahead.

Now, I know what you're thinking. Not everyone has tens of thousands of dollars to give to charity every year. Most people live in families like the ones I grew up around—families who have a tight monthly budget, and often have to stretch one paycheck to make that budget work.

That's why you'll be glad to hear that giving, at least the kind that I'm talking about, has very little to do with money. In fact, it has very little to do with material goods at all. At its core, the act of giving is about time, love, and commitment.

Time, when you think about it, is the most valuable thing you have. After all, time is the one thing in our world that isn't renewable. Once you spend it, you can't get it back. One of the most important things you can do in your life is spending time with others, letting them know they're important to you. Showing unconditional love to your spouse—which is hard and foreign but can be the ultimate game changer—can be among the most rewarding things in the world.

As someone who's been on the other side of unconditional spousal love *a lot* lately, let me tell you that it's always much appreciated.

But you can also help your family members and stop to give detailed answers when your kids ask you questions.

Again, this is made up of small moments.

Get those right, and everything else will fall right into place.

Besides, you're already hardwired to like giving, or to help people.

Imagine something for a moment. You're sitting at home, getting ready to leave for the office. You get a call from a friend whose son is looking to get into the same business you're in. He wants to know if he can take you out to breakfast sometime soon and ask you a few questions about what you do and how you like it.

Wasn't your first reaction to say yes right away and tell the kid everything you know?

I'm sure it was.

And if it wasn't, think back on all the people who helped *you* out when they had no good reason to—the ones who gave you a shot even when the interview didn't go very well, or who took time to explain an industry that you didn't understand even though they had better things to do.

Why did they do that? It probably wasn't because they were hoping the investment in you would pay off someday—although maybe it was. It was because people like to be useful to other people. We like giving our time if we can make other people happy.

So, get out there and do it.

HAVE INTEGRITY

"The man who lies to himself and listens to
his own lie comes to a point that he cannot
distinguish the truth within him, or around him,
and so loses all respect for himself and for others.
And having no respect he ceases to love."

—FYODOR DOSTOEVSKY

As I write these words, I'm coming up on my sixtieth birthday—
which, oddly enough, falls on January 6. You can imagine how
much fun I'm going to have every year for the rest of my life,
blowing out the candles and thinking, once again, about how my
former boss almost tore the Constitution to shreds and sent a mob
of his supporters up to the Capitol building to take over the nation.

Hey, maybe I deserve it.

Anyway, the reason I bring up my birthday at all is that in
recent years, I've had people tell me that I don't look quite as old as
I am. That's not a humble-brag or anything, just something that's
been happening to me. I'll admit, of course, that it usually happens
when I'm doing something over a webcam, which makes it a little
harder to notice my dyed hair and the heavy wrinkles that five kids
have suddenly made appear on my once baby-soft skin.

It happened for the first time a few years ago, when I mentioned on a podcast that I was about to turn fifty-eight. I could tell that the hosts were surprised. When they asked why I didn't look like some of the other guys in their late fifties they'd interviewed, I gave my standard answer.

"Act young, feel young, think young, *be* young."

That might sound cute, but it's true.

When you live like shit, you're going to start looking like shit. That's why most old liars, cheaters, and crooks you know end up fat and bald, while good people usually maintain a youthful energy until they're well into their old age.

Living right is good for you. It keeps you young. When I was growing up, my parents would call it "living with integrity." It means being honest with people even when it's uncomfortable, and trying to see the best in everyone you meet. Sometimes, it means admitting you've made a horrible mistake, or choosing to do the right thing despite knowing that it's going to hurt you in the short term. Like most things, living with integrity is largely about having self-discipline. You need to be able to tell yourself that although the wrong thing—whether it be lying, slacking off, or keeping a secret from someone—might be beneficial to you in the short term, it's not going to be good for you in the long term.

Now, integrity is a strange word. Although we mostly use it today as a synonym for honesty, it's about much more than that. The word, which comes into English from Old French and Latin, refers more to "soundness, wholeness, and completeness." When you have integrity, your spirit is intact. You're whole. You've got a walled fortress around your values and your beliefs, and you don't allow temptation to breach those walls and make you act in ways that you know are wrong.

Like most things we've discussed so far, it's not a binary thing. It's not like people have integrity or don't. It's something that you—and other people—can work at every day. Integrity is about a series of small decisions, which over time make up who you are as a person. If you're faced with a dozen small choices in a day and you choose to do the right thing in nine of them, then you had a pretty good day, integrity-wise. Crack a beer and enjoy being a moral superstar.

You'll have days when that doesn't happen, of course. Days when you can't take the pain of telling people the hard, unvarnished truth, and so you soften things in a way you shouldn't, or you tell someone a small lie that you don't think is going to come back to bite you in the ass. Maybe if you have those days occasionally, you'll be fine. Maybe you will get away with slightly misrepresenting the content of a deal, or with selling someone a product that you know isn't *really* as good as you've led them to believe it is.

But in my experience, you'll always get caught. Eventually, the small lies you've told will catch up with you, and the people you've cheated will show up in your life again and cheat you right back twice as bad. That's when you'll start to develop some serious bags under your eyes because you're not sleeping as well as you would have if you'd just told the truth. It's when people start looking surprised when you tell them your age, and not in a good way.

Trust me. When you tell the truth, don't cheat people, and live with integrity at every moment, you'll age gracefully. If you *do* cheat people, it'll catch up with you. Unlike Dorian Gray, you don't have a picture in the attic that ages every time you do a bad thing. It might take a while, but the things you've done will eventually show up on your face.

Especially when it comes to dishonesty.

➤ ➤ ➤

Look, don't lie. It's never a good thing.

For about eleven days, I worked for a guy who lied all the time. When you asked him who was coming to a meeting, he'd lie to you. When you asked whether he'd read the full text of a report that his intel agencies had prepared for him, he'd lie.

Eventually, as I'm sure you know, things got to a point where President Trump wasn't even lying to protect himself anymore. He was doing it because he didn't know any other way. He was saying one thing even though he'd said exactly the opposite just a few days earlier. According to the *Washington Post*, which admittedly had a crazy bias against the guy from day one, President Trump told 30,573 lies during his time in the White House. These lies covered every subject you could possibly imagine.

In the first hundred days, we had 492 lies. Given these numbers, he was lying five times a day.

During my very short stint in the building, I heard the guy direct people to tell dozens of lies on his behalf. Although I'm happy to report that as the communications director, I managed to get out without ever having to say one thing to the press that I didn't believe was true at the time. Even my assertion that President Trump had done great things for the country during his first few years in office—which included lowering tax rates, raising incomes, and making the country a better place to do business—was something I believed one hundred percent at the time it left my mouth. Even after all that's transpired between me and former President Trump, I *still* believe that he and his administration managed to do some great things during their first two years in office. If he could have tempered his worst instincts a little, he could have done even more amazing things.

But after I left, the lies kept getting bigger. As you probably know if you've ever tried to keep a lie going—and honestly, who hasn't?—this is what happens. You start to build little networks of lies, and then those lies start to crash into one another and create new lies. You can't say one thing because it contradicts what you said yesterday, even though the thing you want to say today is true and the thing you said yesterday wasn't. You start having to keep a mental inventory of every sentence that leaves your mouth so that you don't say something in the future that reveals you for the lazy, lying POS that you are.

Aside from being morally wrong, it's exhausting.

Not to mention that the results can be devastating.

Consider what happened in the weeks following the election of 2020, during which I campaigned my ass off to ensure Trump got out of the White House and retired to Florida as soon as humanly possible. Despite clear evidence that he'd lost, President Trump refused to concede. For years, pundits had been raising the possibility that this guy would, when defeated, simply deny reality and pretend he'd actually won. Most people didn't believe he was *that* insane. Even I wasn't sure.

But those who knew him best knew exactly what was coming. They had seen evidence that he was willing to deny even basic reality—or at least pretend to—knowing that he had a gullible audience of people who'd bought his bullshit hook, line, and sinker. Even when the stakes were the highest they could possibly be, and the fate of democracy itself hung in the balance, the guy would not stop lying. We were warned by Alexander Vindman, who said, "It is improper for the president of the United States to demand a foreign government investigate a U.S. citizen and political opponent." We were warned by Fiona Hill, who said, "Not once did I see him do anything to put America first. Not once, not for a single second."

They knew that someone who lies about the little things will usually lie about the big things, too. This guy, they knew, wasn't going to develop a sense of integrity when the stakes got as high as they've ever been for him. If anything, the opposite was going to happen.

Some of these people had known Donald Trump since way back in the day, when he was dialing into radio talk shows to lie about all the women he'd slept with and calling reporters to give fake quotes about himself. During these calls, as several reporters have written about, Trump would pretend to be a guy named "John Barron," talking himself up because no one else was willing to do it at the time. You have to be amazed at what it takes to engage in that kind of lie. Think about the steps involved. First, you must think of the fake name. Then the fake quote. Then you have to dial the phone and say the words out loud. Any normal person would be embarrassed before they could even pick up the landline and start dialing.

But as we've seen repeatedly, there are people like Trump who don't feel the same sense of shame that the rest of us do. That, in my opinion, is a big part of what allowed him to make it so far in the American political system. He was simply willing to eat more shit than anyone else, and then lie about what he'd really done straight to the faces of the American people and the press. Then he'd attack anyone who tried to correct him. When it finally came down to the facts—when it was absolutely certain that there was no way he could wriggle out of it—he'd just shake off the lie like it didn't matter.

And sadly, to most of his supporters, it really didn't matter.

This isn't new either. If you're looking to understand the psyche of our forty-fifth president, there are many books—and, I'm sure, many more to come—that probe his motivations and tell his life story. One of the finest I've ever read is *Commander in Cheat*, written by a longtime *Sports Illustrated* writer named Rick Reilly who'd taken on Trump as a subject in the past. The book's main thesis is that if you want to get to know Donald Trump—or any powerful man, for that matter—you need only look at the way he plays golf. A person's golf game, as Reilly puts it, won't show you *everything* about a person, but it'll reveal the most important aspects of their personality.

Near the beginning of the book, Reilly tells a story about meeting Trump for the first time while he was writing a cover story about him for *Sports Illustrated*. It was the early '90s, and Reilly was a staff writer for the magazine.

But that didn't stop Trump from introducing him to everyone they came across on the golf course as everything *but* a writer for the magazine he worked for.

"Trump didn't' just lie nonstop about himself that day," Reilly writes. "He lied nonstop about ME. He'd go up to some member and say, 'This is Rick. He's the president of *Sports Illustrated*.' The guy would reach out to shake my hesitant hand, but by then Trump had dragged me forward to the next member. Or secretary. Or chef. 'This is Rick. He publishes *Sports Illustrated*.' Before I could object, he'd go, 'And this is Chef. He was voted best hamburger chef in the world!' And the poor chef would look at me and shake his head with a helpless 'no,' same as me. When we were alone, I finally said, 'Donald, why are you lying about me?' 'Sounds better,' he said."

Now that we're on the other side of Donald Trump's first—and only, I hope—term in office, we're used to hearing these kinds of lies from him. But back then, it was still shocking that someone could be so brazenly loose with the truth. What was even more shocking at the time was that almost everyone in the world *knew* that Trump was a liar, and they'd allow him to lie in the pages of their newspapers and magazines, and eventually on their network airtime, anyway.

"Sounding better," as Reilly puts it, "is Trump's m.o. It colors everything he says and does. The truth doesn't break an egg with Trump. It's all about how it sounds, how it looks, and the fact checkers can go run a 100-yard dash in a 50-yard gym."

By the end of his book, Reilly succeeds in making the case that Trump, who routinely cheats at golf and lies about his prowess in the game, is not someone you should trust to be in charge of anything. Sure, he might get away with telling white lies for a while. He might even get away with telling *massive* lies, even in full view of "fact checkers" and the best reporters in the world, and never quite feel the sting.

But eventually, those lies will form a web that even big fat Trump can't wriggle himself out of. In some sense, that happened in the aftermath of the 2020 election, when the guy's lies about winning the election caught up to him in the form of many hundreds of psychos storming the Capitol on his behalf—an event that made him completely unelectable in the eyes of many Americans, all but ensuring that he wouldn't be able to attain power again. Of course, maybe I'm wrong, and the day that this guy is crushed by the weight of his accumulated untruths is still to come.

But it is coming.

And the most important part, (the reason I've been going on about this for so long), is that it all started small. It began with little white lies about the size of his buildings and the amount of money in his checking account. Then it moved to more absurd things, such as claiming that the sixth floor of Trump Tower was actually the fourteenth floor. (Floors numbers six through thirteen don't actually exist; he cut them out so he could sell all the apartments above as if they were much higher off the street than they were.) Then we got the cheating at golf, the lying about hurricane patterns, and the burning classified documents in the White House fireplace.

There are some people in the world who'll tell you that people can separate parts of their lives, acting upright and proper in one part but being a complete scumbag in another. It's a myth that gained currency in our culture thanks, at least in part, to mafia movies. Watching films like *Goodfellas* and *The Godfather*, you see men who do illegal things (and kill people) but also do great things for the neighborhood and love their families. Sure, they shoot guys in the back of the head, but they also have a rigid code of honor when it comes to their personal lives.

I think it's bullshit.

If I've learned anything in my (almost) six decades on earth, it's that almost all the time, the way you do some things is the way you do everything.

Let me repeat that: *The way you do some things is how you do everything.*

In other words, if you're going to lie about your crowd size and how many floors are in your building, you're not going to suddenly stop lying when it comes to a presidential election or your illegal retention of classified documents. If you're willing to cheat on your wife or lie to your kids, you'll probably cheat me in a deal and lie to your business partners.

But the opposite is also true. If you're honest about the small things—admitting when you screw up even when you could easily wriggle out of the situation with a lie—I'll know you can be trusted with the big things. When I hire someone new—especially someone I don't know very well—I'm always on the lookout for integrity. That doesn't mean I want you to do everything perfectly right away, or to come up with a million great ideas during your first hour on the job. I just want to know that you handle yourself well, and that integrity is important to you. That begins, almost all the time, with honesty.

So, my advice? Be a straight shooter. Tell the truth even when it's painful, because failing to be truthful will *always* come back to bite you. I know that I'm telling you things your mother probably told you when you were like five years old, but there's a reason she told you those things. She was a smart lady.

I've also personally experienced the benefits of being a straight shooter. My whole life, despite having many (*many*) faults, I have managed to stay honest. I'm good about admitting when I screw up, and I don't keep secrets from people I care about. I might not always like the immediate outcomes, but it's always served me well in the long term. If you have integrity, there will always be opportunity.

Take this recent blowup, for example.

If you've followed the story about FTX and Sam Bankman-Fried closely, you might know that I was a big supporter of the enterprise for a while. I mean a *big*, sell-thirty-percent-of-my-company-to-FTX, introduce-the-dude-to-all-my-friends-and-try-to-drum-up-business-for-him kind of supporter.

It was not, to put it mildly, my finest moment. In fact, it might be the *least* fine moment of my career thus far, including the one that made me the butt of every late-night joke in the country.

Look. I had several conversations with the guy early on that led me to believe he truly wanted the best for the world, and that he was going to operate with integrity to bring his lofty goals to fruition. I appreciated that he seemed to be a straight shooter, and that he was a simple guy. I liked the fact that despite having billions of dollars in the bank, he still drove a modest car and dressed like he still lived in a dorm room. As someone who aspires to modesty myself—and sure, often fails miserably at it—I was instantly drawn to the man the media had dubbed "SBF."

So, I went to the Middle East with Sam. I introduced him to friends there, in Riyadh, Dubai, and Abu Dhabi. I often vouched for him, putting the full weight of my reputation and friendships behind my recommendation that my new friends do business with the guy.

I did this because I believed strongly in the ability of cryptocurrency to remake the world. I still do. The technology will de-layer transactions and take out intermediaries. This sort of cost savings will lead to both more economic innovation and efficiency.

As with most new technologies, though, there were going to be some bumps in the road. There certainly were with SBF. Unbeknownst to me, the company this guy was running was one big fraud. And it wasn't an accidental fraud either, which can happen sometimes when you're dealing with a brand new technology and building a big business at the same time. This guy knew—and three of his associates knew—that what they were doing with the two companies under their control was not above board. But they knew how to hide the bad shit and fudge the balance sheets in such a way that even the best, most accomplished venture funds and sovereign wealth funds, who are trained to spot this sort of thing from a mile away, couldn't detect anything.

In the year since the collapse of FTX, I've taken a lot of heat for encouraging my friends, customers, and colleagues to believe in this company. I still have podcast hosts and news reporters asking me whether I feel bad about having done this. In the minds of my critics, I knowingly—or at least, not *un*knowingly—misrepresented the credibility of SBF because I stood to make money on the deal.

Two problems there. First, it's not like I was selling them something I wasn't prepared to try myself. While I was flying around with SBF and vouching for him to my friends and colleagues, I was also cutting a deal that would give him 30 percent of my company with the right to buy the remaining shares over the next three years.

If FTX was a bowl of poison pasta, I was right there at the table with everyone else, filling my plate and preparing to chow down.

Second, not one of the meetings we had actually resulted in more investment for FTX. Which is a great thing, considering what was going on behind the scenes.

Sadly, the saga of Sam Bankman-Fried is another great example of what happens when you don't live your life with integrity. It also illustrates how when it comes to integrity, the small things are what matter. You can go around to every newspaper in the country talking about how you're going to use all your money to fix the world, save the rainforests, and treat everyone in the country to a free ice cream party every Friday for the remainder of your life. But if you're being dishonest behind the scenes—even about things that you think are small, or that you truly believe you can iron out in the future—you can't say that you're living with integrity.

These days, it's very easy to cover up your small acts of dishonesty with big acts of charity and magnanimity. In fact, it's usually the biggest liars in the world who talk the biggest game about how they're doing the right thing, saving the world, and bringing society forward with their work. They do this even when they're charged with crimes and standing trial for fraud and corruption on a mass scale.

In fact, sometimes being morally upstanding—or at least believing you are—makes things much worse. If you haven't seen it, I would recommend watching the documentary *The Inventor: Out for Blood in Silicon Valley*, which chronicles the rise and fall of Elizabeth Holmes, founder of the fraudulent startup Theranos. As many media outlets have pointed out in recent years—especially after Holmes was sentenced to eleven years in prison—the parallels between Theranos and FTX are stunning. Both founders were charismatic media darlings who were taken in by big-time Democratic politicians. Both were a little strange, but people were willing to overlook their personality quirks because of how amazing the technology they were pushing seemed to be.

Most importantly, both people believed they were doing a wonderful thing for the world. They both believed they were acting with integrity. In the case of Elizabeth Holmes, Theranos was going to make it possible for people to conduct blood tests for hundreds of diseases using a small machine in their homes. Her technology was going to revolutionize the healthcare industry, and it was going to save lives. During presentations, she often told the heartwarming story of her uncle, who was diagnosed with skin cancer that became brain and bone cancer.

FROM WALL STREET TO THE WHITE HOUSE AND BACK

At this point, the crowd would break out in *oohs* and *awws*, just in time for Holmes to declare that her company would "ensure that people didn't have to say goodbye so early."

It was the perfect way to get away with fraud. Convince people that what you're doing is noble, and they'll be much less likely to ask questions. This is because they want to believe that good things are possible. Meanwhile, the person who's committing the fraud, telling lies every day, also needs to justify it to herself. So do the other people who know that something is not quite right with the tech or the business model.

They're able to do this, according to the behavioral economist Dan Ariely, who's been studying this sort of thing at Duke University for decades, because of an in-built mechanism in our brains—one that allows us to justify bad behavior under the right circumstances.

In the documentary, Ariely describes an experiment that he once conducted in his laboratory. This experiment, which is quite complicated, was meant to study what happens inside people's heads when they lie. The results, as he describes them in *The Inventor*, are shocking.

"The experiment," according to an excellent summary written by a reporter named Jon Miltimore, involves "a six-sided die."

It goes like this:

> [Researchers] had participants roll for a monetary reward corresponding to the number on the die. If the die landed on the number 4, the individual was paid $4; if they rolled a 6, they'd receive $6. Before rolling, however, participants were asked to decide which side of the die—bottom or top—determined the dollar amount they'd receive. Participants were

told to not tell the researchers their choice, but to mark this on a piece of paper. Essentially, participants could make more money by simply lying—and that's what many did.

"When people [rolled] 20 times, we found that they were incredibly lucky," said Ariely. "Not lucky 100 percent of the time, but maybe 13 or 14 times."

His experiment did not end there, however. Ariely conducted the same experiment, but with people connected to a lie detector. Did people still cheat? Yes, and the lie detector confirms this. (Not always and not perfectly, Ariely concedes.) But the real twist comes when researchers conducted the same experiment but told participants the money they earn will be donated to a charity of their choice.

What happens?

"People cheat more," Ariely says. "And the lie detector stops working."

Did you get all that?

I'll admit that it took me a few times to understand exactly what was going on the first time I saw the film. It was even harder to write down a summary of the experiment (which is why I ended up borrowing from Miltimore, who did a much better job than I ever could).

But once I internalized the truth of what Ariely and his team had uncovered, I felt a chill run up my spine. Every day, you encounter people who are lying to you. Most of them feel bad about doing this, which is why you can usually spot a liar. You can detect a little flop sweat and feel some tension in the room when they speak. You might notice their eyes are darting around the room, or that their hands get sweaty when they shake yours.

Those are the people who are lying for the classic reasons: because they're greedy, or because they just want to screw with you.

But there are other people in the world who believe they're complexly justified in lying straight to your face. They believe this, in most cases, because they think the cause they're lying for— whether it's a company they just started or a political candidate they support—is worthy. As we've seen in the experiment that Ariely and his colleagues carried out at Duke, the belief that you're acting for a good cause effectively *shuts down* the part of your brain that makes you feel bad about lying. It makes you feel like you can do whatever you want and still claim to have integrity.

But you can't. At its core, having integrity is not about grand narratives of human progress, and it's not about the net effect that your life is going to have on the planet after you die. You don't get to weigh up all the good things and bad things you've done, hoping that your bad actions will lead to enough good for enough to people to make up for the fact that you lied to people. That math is never going to work out.

Integrity is about the small things, just like discipline. It's about judging what's right in every moment, and then doing that thing even though it might cause you a small amount of pain. When you make the mistake, admit it. When you have the chance to lie and make a little money, fully believing that no one's ever going to find out, don't do it.

I don't know why I didn't spot SBF's lies a mile away. Maybe it's because he believed what he was doing was good for the world, which made him a phenomenal con artist. Maybe it's because *I* wanted to believe that the deal I was cutting with him was going to work out. It certainly would have been good for the cryptocurrency industry, which I'm still incredibly bullish on, and will be long after this book goes out of print.

But I do know that his story proves my case. At any point along the way, he could have alerted the people in his company that they had major problems. If he did it early enough, he could have taken a few temporary losses, scaled some things back, and figured out a way to fix things. That would have meant a little less money in the short term, and it probably would have meant some bad press. He probably wouldn't have been invited to as many parties as he'd been before.

But he would have been able to look his employees in their eyes and know that he was running a good business, and that he was doing so with integrity.

Instead, he allowed the lies to build. One day, they came crashing down on top of him, leaving only a pair of hairy legs and sandals sticking out from under the pile.

Let that be a lesson to anyone who thinks dishonesty—even the momentary kind, and even when it's for a great cause—is a good strategy in this life.

It's not.

➤ ➤ ➤

As for me? Look, I've already said I'm not the greatest guy in the world, morals-wise. My worst sins are the kinds of things I'm not going to print in this book. But beyond those, I do the usual annoying things. I leave the toilet seat up in my house sometimes.

I jaywalk. I walk past people who want me to sign petitions to get elephants out of zoos and pretend I don't hear them.

But I don't lie, and I don't cheat people.

That's why I'm still walking around, running businesses, and having a great time while most people who got caught up in the FTX business are in big trouble. The same goes for my friend Kevin O'Leary, who also got in on the deal.

Did we both take baths?

Sure.

Did we fuck up big time?

You betcha.

But we can walk around knowing we did the right thing, and that everyone who's entrusted us with their money is in much better shape than they would be if they didn't.

That's a good feeling.

Now, one more note about honesty. In addition to being good business for moral reasons, it's also the safest way to go from a practical standpoint.

Let me explain. On a purely selfish level, being honest with people gives you a great deal of cover for your other shortcomings.

Make a business mistake? Fine. People will forgive you if you're honest about them. Don't really know what you're doing? Great! No one does when they first start out. As long as you don't try to pretend you know more than you do—as I did many times in my mid-twenties, usually to devastating results—people will be more than willing to teach you.

The bottom line is that being honest, and living with integrity at every moment, will pay off in the long run, even if it seems to hurt in the present.

So, go tell someone the truth today. Ask a stupid question. And please, don't try to pretend to be something you're not.

And remember: honesty and integrity always lead to more opportunity.

✍ Lesson 12

FINISH
WHAT YOU START

"You learn by finishing things."

—Neil Gaiman

Almost every time I speak in public, I'll allow some time for a Q-and-A session at the end of my remarks. That means that even if I bore people to tears, they'll feel like they got their money's worth at the end. One of the questions I get the most during these sessions is what advice I have for young people who want to get into the business I'm in.

Luckily, I've got a lot of that. You're reading a book full of all the things I would say if I had the time.

But I don't always have the time. So, I boil it down to something simple: *Finish what you start.* In the early days of starting a company—or inventing a product, or writing a book, or even completing a basic task—a fear of failure often sets in. That fear can be paralyzing. Your inner voice tells you that you're a fraud, you're no good, and that you were crazy even to *begin* to think you could pull this off.

Don't listen.

Finish things even if they're bad. Even if you hate what you see at the end of the day, keep plugging along.

Of course, this is much easier said than done. So is everything I've said in this book, which, you won't be surprised to learn, has been much easier to write than some of my other ones.

In fact, some of the most talented people in the world—people whose books we read and whose songs we know, whose products we use and whose names we hold up as models of hard work, grit, and determination—have found themselves deep into a project, staring at a half-finished paragraph or PowerPoint slide, and having absolutely no idea how to keep going.

One of the best expressions of what this is like came in 1970, when the songwriter Paul Simon went on a television program called *The Dick Cavett Show* and talked about the process he often used to write his hit songs. Specifically, he was talking about "Bridge Over Troubled Water," a song that was already a megahit by the time he sat on Dick Cavett's couch with an acoustic guitar.

For a few minutes, he said, the song came easily. He knew exactly what chords came next, and he got the words for the first verse in almost the time it took to sing them out loud.

Then, when it came time to figure out a chorus, he had nothing.

"I was stuck," he said.

When Dick Cavett asked what exactly Paul Simon meant by "stuck," he thought for a moment. Then, finally, he said, "Well, everywhere I went led me where I didn't want to be. So, I was stuck."

If you've ever been stuck—in your career, on a creative project, or in life and general—you probably know the feeling. Every time you make a move that you think is going to lead you out of whatever dark hole you're in, you end up either right back where you started or in an even deeper hole than you were in before. It doesn't take long for all the negative self-talk to make the situation worse. You start to notice that nothing you've been doing to resolve your situation is working. That makes you discouraged. Before long, you start to believe you're the kind of person who can't do anything right.

But that kind of self-talk is almost never right.

The only way to get around it is to realize that the feeling of being stuck—of being unable to connect one idea to another, or to think your way out of whatever problem you're in—is always temporary. What's happening isn't a loss of creative faculties. It's not a problem of ability.

Usually, it's because the two sides of you—the actor and the critic—are not getting along.

Think of your brain like a big machine that's run by two little guys. One of these guys is the one who does things, builds things, and makes decisions. This is the "actor." When you sit down to work, he's the one who comes up with all the ideas, follows the weird threads, and makes connections between things that don't seem to go together.

He makes shit happen, in other words.

Working in the same space, you have the critic. This is the guy who'll tell the actor when he's going nuts, or when something he's come up with is terrible. Every time the actor tries to go down a bad path, the critic pulls him back and lets him know that it's time to start over.

In some brains, the critic is very mild-mannered. He doesn't speak up often. If you need an example, look no further than Kanye West. Whatever that guy thinks, it comes right out of his mouth. That's why he's able to make such great music, combining elements in a way that would never occur to a normal person. It's why his lyrics are so strange, and the beats underneath them seem to come from another universe. If there's a critic in there—someone telling Kanye to pull back, think about something for a little longer, or slow down—it's a *very* quiet one.

For the most part, this has worked out for Kanye. His music is beloved. He was a mogul in the clothing space. I don't think anyone can talk about the history of hip-hop music without mentioning his name at least once. But the lack of an internal critic, as I'm sure you've noticed, has also been…let's say, not so great for the guy.

I don't think anyone would disagree that he could have used a little more self-criticism when he blamed members of a certain religion for all his problems, for instance, or when he stormed the stage to grab an award from poor Taylor Swift.

But he's an extreme guy.

On the other side, you have people whose editor is so loud that they find it extremely difficult to get anything done. To stay in the hip-hop genre, think about Dr. Dre. Despite having just as much talent as Kanye West, Dr. Dre has put out half as many albums. His friends attribute this to his "perfectionism." He sits in his studio all day, putting together instrumental tracks and vocals, but doesn't finish or release any of it. One artist that Dr. Dre worked with claimed that he made him record the same vocal take five hundred times, and then didn't even release the song.

Maybe that is perfectionism. Of course, as Winston Churchill once said, another way to spell "perfectionism" is "P-A-R-A-L-Y-S-I-S." When your inner critic is too loud, you can get blocked up. You'll stop doing imperfect work, sure, but you'll also stop doing the work that leads you to the good work.

You can also look at Harper Lee, author of *To Kill a Mockingbird*. She wrote that book in just a few years, and then never did anything again. Maybe it's because she felt that everything she had to say was contained in that single book, but I doubt it. I think it's much more likely that she was afraid to set anything down after enjoying such massive success. The critic in her head, in other words, was much louder and more active than the actor.

The first step to finishing what we start is to recognize that getting stuck is not a product of not knowing what you're doing. Rather, it's the product of not *liking* what you're doing. It happens when the critic in your head is beating up on the actor.

For centuries, people have been trying to find ways to fix this problem, and they all boil down to the same thing.

Keep going and fix it later.

For the best examples of this, we can look to the world of literature.

If I've learned anything since I've been hosting my podcast *Open Book*, it's that publishing is a tough business. Although many of the big-name authors I've spoken with do just fine for themselves— Don Winslow or Robert Greene, for instance—most authors need a second job to support their writing habit. The audiences for books, especially long novels, has been getting smaller every year, and prestige television is getting harder to compete with as well. I'm sure I don't have to tell you that sitting down and binging three episodes of *Succession* is a lot easier than getting all the way through the latest novel on your shelf.

But if you speak with people who've been successful in this business for a long time, you learn something very important about success—namely that it almost never comes all at once. It comes, rather, from spending many days working at the same thing, and doing it steadily.

Stephen King, one of the most successful authors of all time, wakes up every morning and writes ten pages. He does this on Christmas, his birthday, and even Halloween, (which I would imagine, having read a few of his books, is probably a big holiday in his house). Other writers do fewer than ten pages—which, as anyone who's ever tried to get a story down on paper can tell you, is still a *lot* of pages—but they all, with almost no exceptions, get up and do something every day.

As the writer Anne Lamott once put it, all you need to do is a couple of crappy pages every day. Do that, and after a few months, you'll end up with a big stack. *Then*, your inner critic can get to work and decide how to fix it.

In other words, you can fix bad work; but you can't fix no work.

Perhaps more than any other profession, writing is about consistency. There are days when even the most brilliant novelists in the world can't think of a single word. But they know that getting to the end of a book takes discipline, and that nothing is going to get written unless they shut up and write it.

That means ignoring emails. It means putting off vacations and refusing to stay out late the night before a big writing day. Sometimes, it means sitting down all morning and fighting the urge to get up and do something else until your body is literally shaking.

At first, this is painful. But it yields amazing results. That's why the Germans have the word *Sitzfleisch*, which means "ass in chair." Walking around and thinking about all the great ideas you have for books—or companies, or foundations, or podcasts—is not going to get you anywhere. Sitting around at the coffee shop and talking with your friends about all the cool things you're going to do someday is not going to get you anywhere either. The only thing that's going to get you anywhere is blocking out time, sitting down, and getting some work done.

That is why when you ask most professional writers what they do about the dreaded disease known as "writer's block," they'll usually laugh in your face. This is because in the eyes of people who put words on paper for a living—the ones who come up with the stories we all want to read and then write them down, often over the course of many years—there's no such thing as "writer's block." Sure, there are days when you get up and don't feel like working, when the ideas don't seem to be flowing and everything you do looks horrible. But if you're a professional, you push through those days and do something anyway.

The same is true for any endeavor, even in the business world. When you've got your eye on a goal that's a few hundred miles away—say, the moment when you shake hands and close a deal— you'll often find that it's hard to get up every day and put in the small work necessary to get things done.

But when you only focus on what's in front of you—putting one word after the other, or making one phone call at a time—you'll find that the end comes much sooner than you thought it would.

So, get to the end. Then worry about fixing what you've done.

✐ Lesson 13

...BUT KNOW WHEN TO QUIT

Sometimes, when the going gets tough—when it seems like you can't possibly send another email, make another phone call, or write another word—you have to dig deep and find the inspiration that made you start in the first place. Sometimes you have to close your eyes, ball up your fists, and find the kind of inner strength you didn't even know existed to keep you going until you hit your goal. You have to crank some AC/DC on the stereo, watch a few motivational YouTube clips from Navy SEALs, and push through the pain or the creative block until you're done.

Other times, though, when the going gets tough, you just have to quit.

Step back, shrug your shoulders, get an ice cream cone, and quit.

Now, I know this isn't advice that you'll find in most self-help books currently on the market. *Drop Everything and Give Up* or *Fuck it, Let's Go Home* don't quite have the same ring to them as the titles of books that encourage you to keep fighting, dig deep, and finish your tasks without complaining. But I don't think you cracked the cover on this book thinking I was a drill sergeant,

134

(which is good, because I'm about the furthest thing from it that you can possibly be).

In fact, over the course of my life, I've found that giving up is often a great solution.

Under the right conditions, of course.

Think about whatever you're trying to accomplish like it's a road race. Let's say a 5k for charity. Sometimes, when your body starts telling you it's time quit at the two-mile marker, you need to push through the pain and run the next mile even if it feels like you're going to die. Sometimes, as we've covered in the lesson about discipline, the mind needs to take over and tell the body who's in charge. This is when pushing past our limits, however painful that process might be, leads us to good things—bigger muscles, greater stamina, or a product we're proud of.

However.

There are times when you start to slow down at the two-mile mark because your shin bone is slowly breaking apart, or because you had a little too much to drink last night and taking even two more steps is going to send your body into dangerous levels of dehydration. There are also times when you feel completely up to the task of finishing the race, but you know there's a family of angry bears up ahead, and that you probably can't run faster than they can.

So, the question becomes: How do I tell the difference?

I'm glad you asked because you're not the first one to do so.

For as long as people have been writing things down, they've been obsessed with the limits of human performance. If you don't believe me, think about the first guy to ever run a marathon, a race that was invented to honor Pheidippides, who in 490 BC ran twenty-six miles after the battle of Marathon to notify his other Greek citizens that they need more reinforcements. Then he fell over and died.

Now, this could be a myth, but in honor of his spirit, the first modern marathon took place at the 1896 Olympic Games in Athens.

So, that's why they call it that. Because that's the distance the guy happened to run before he fell over and died.

Now, I'm not sure what the moral of that story is. To be honest, I'm not even sure there is one. But if I had to make something up, I would say that it's probably something along the lines of: Unless you need to warn people of an advancing army, there's no need to keep running until you die. Take a break. Regroup. Try again tomorrow.

As with most things, it's difficult to tell when you've reached the point at which you need to quit. How do you know whether the obstacle in front of you is a brick wall that you should bust through like the Kool-Aid Man or a steel wall that you couldn't get through even with the most expensive, high-tech tools in the world?

It's not easy. But it is doable.

Some of the best advice I've ever heard about quitting comes from a small book called *The Dip*, written by the marketing guru Seth Godin. Although this book is short, it contains valuable advice about when (and how) to quit something that isn't going to work out for you in the long run.

The first thing to figure out is whether you're panicking. If you're in a bad headspace, worrying about money or your reputation to the detriment of clear thinking, don't do anything. Wait until you've got a clear head, and then start thinking again.

Once you've done that, according to Godin, you need to figure out whether quitting is going to benefit you in the long run. To do that, look at your current situation. Really think about whether pushing through the momentary blocks is going to put you in a better situation. If you spend weeks fixing the problem in front of you, are you going to come out the other side better than you were before?

Or are you in a cul-de-sac, a situation in which no amount of work is going to push you forward? If this is the case, then now is the time to quit. Do it strategically, and do it so that you can't go back on the decision. This is known as "strategic quitting," and it's incredibly important.

Strategic quitting isn't about giving up at the first sign of trouble. It's about understanding that our time, energy, and resources are finite and that to achieve our goals, we must direct them where they're most effective—even if that means abandoning a path we've already started down. It's about realizing that the biggest failure isn't in quitting, but in persisting in a situation with no potential for success.

As usual, the advice that I've given you so far in this section applies not only to business, passion projects, and your career, but also to your interactions with other people.

As we've seen—and will continue to see—in the pages of this book, people are usually better than you think. That's why you should be careful about whom you decide to fight with. In my experience, the more you speak to someone—even if you're speaking in a vitriolic, antagonistic manner—the more you'll start to like that person. This is because the more you listen to someone speak, the more you become aware of what that person has in common with you.

Think about it. If you're in the middle of the most brutal business negotiation of your life, and the other guy is going on and on (and on, and on) about what an asshole you are, and he swears on his kid's life that he's going to ruin you financially if you don't agree to his terms, you still learned that he had kids. Then, you start thinking about how he probably loves his kids just as much as you love yours. Then, maybe he insults you with a turn of phrase that you think is funny. Maybe he uses a line that you've used a few times before, and you realize that you got it from the same old sitcom that you both like.

Maybe that doesn't happen often. But when it does, you'll realize that people are mostly good. With very few exceptions, we all want the same things, and we usually don't want to make other people miserable. There's no point. We all love our families, we want to make them happy, and we want our favorite sports teams to win. The things that make us fight with one another, mostly politics and religion, turn out not to matter as much as you think.

Sometimes, though, you have to stop trying and tell someone to go pound sand. In my experience, these interactions happen much less frequently than you'd think (especially considering how much time I've spent in the world of cutthroat business and politics).

But they do happen.

A year or two ago, I went on a podcast with two guys who called themselves the "Drinking Bros." We had a good conversation for about ninety minutes. Then, toward the end of the interview, they started talking about how they weren't going to get the Covid-19 vaccine, which had just been unveiled at the time we were speaking. They said they were healthy, that they didn't need it, and they'd rather take their chances with Covid.

I tried to be polite about things, disagreeing and saying that I would have all my employees get the vaccine. I noted that unless we all came together as a nation and stopped listening to people who wanted to divide us, we were going to be in big trouble.

If my memory serves me right, they started cursing at me, letting me know I was an idiot, and saying other things that I hadn't heard in quite some time. It's not like I'm unused to that kind of talk, but there's only so much that even I can take.

So, I hung up and gave a little back to them.

Sometimes, that's the only way to handle these situations.

✎ Lesson 14

KNOW WHO
YOUR BOSS IS

I'm an entrepreneur. If you're reading this book, there's a good chance that you are, too.

When I use that label, of course, I don't just mean that I've filed paperwork to start a business, found customers, and then operated that business for a period of time.

I mean that being an entrepreneur is in my blood. It has been since I was very young.

When people ask me what I mean by this, I'll often tell a story about the paper route I had when I was kid in Port Washington, Long Island. This was the mid-1970s, by the way, and things were not going well with the economy. I vividly remember coming home one day to find my parents arguing at the kitchen table. I couldn't quite tell what they were saying, given that they were speaking in Italian. But I knew we were about to have trouble in the house.

I would later learn that my father had just heard that his hours were being cut. For the past twenty years, he'd been working as a crane operator down at a small construction company in my hometown. While his paycheck had never been massive, he was able to provide his family with everything we needed to survive because he worked his ass off. We always had food on the table, furniture that wasn't falling apart, and air conditioners to cool the place down during the hot, sticky Long Island summers. But there was only so much you could take out of my father's paycheck before we really started to feel the pain.

In the summer of 1974, that's exactly what started to happen. Slowly, my siblings and I realized that we didn't have quite as much as we used to. I'm not saying we were dirt poor or anything, but we didn't go on vacation or get new, name-brand clothes every year.

Fast forward a year, and there I am: little Anthony Scaramucci on his bike working his paper route. I've got thirty-one houses relying on me to get their news every morning. I'm hustling and bringing the money right to my mother. But it's not enough to ease what's going at home, obviously. So, I tell myself I got to do extra. I need more customers.

I come up with this idea. Before going to collect the subscription money for the first paper (think the daily paper) on Wednesdays, I drop off a different free paper (the weekend edition) on Monday. Then, when I go to collect, I ring their doorbell.

"Hello, Mrs. Michalakis, Mr. Michalakis, how are you? Great. Did you get the paper yesterday? I dropped off a free paper for you."

"Yes, I did. Aren't you Marie Scaramucci's son?"

"Why, yes, I am. Oh, by the way, I see that you're not subscribed to the weekend edition. Would you like a daily subscription, which is Monday through Saturday, or a Sunday only?"

I locked up those extra sales. I went from delivering thirty-one papers in a week to ninety almost overnight, without adding any more stops to my route. My revenue exploded, and guess what? I wasn't at the mercy of some foreman. I didn't have to worry about getting my hours cut back. My sense of self was evolving. It felt as if I was rewriting an intergenerational narrative and insulating myself from the possibility of ever feeling the kind of shame my dad must have when he was worried about putting food on our table.

Byron Wien, the legendary Wall Street investor, writes about this. He believes that by the age of eleven, we begin to realize and idolize what our adult lives are going to look like. That vision is, of course, informed by our parents. We begin to sense which parts of their personalities we want to embrace and which we want to shed. As much as I love my dad, I was rejecting his dependence on others for his livelihood—in both the emotional and pragmatic sense of the word—while fully embracing all those Italian sensibilities us Port Washington kids inherit and tend to be so proud of.

Of course, rejecting dependence on other people doesn't mean that you don't have a boss. Everyone has a boss. The key to succeeding is knowing who your boss is, and how to properly interact with that person.

Traditionally, we equate "the boss" with our immediate supervisor or company CEO. However, in a broader, more profound sense, anyone who influences your professional decisions, actions, and performance can be your boss. Indeed, in the interconnected web of modern commerce, everyone from clients to coworkers, stakeholders to consumers, could be wearing the invisible mantle of "the boss."

Understanding and accepting this idea broadens your perspective and amplifies your sense of accountability. It requires recognizing that each interaction, each business decision, each product delivered, has a ripple effect across a vast pool of people—your bosses.

Take, for instance, your customers. They may not sit in a corner office or preside over board meetings, but make no mistake—they are your bosses. They hold your business in their hands, their satisfaction a deciding factor in your success. Every product you design, every service you provide, is ultimately for them. They determine your brand's reputation, its market share, and its bottom line. In this sense, the customer isn't just always right; the customer is your boss.

Similarly, your employees can also be your bosses. Yes, you may determine their tasks, their deadlines, and their remuneration, but they can profoundly influence your company's culture, productivity, and overall success. Employees that are valued, listened to, and respected will often reward you with loyalty, creativity, and exceptional performance. They have the hands-on knowledge of the inner workings of the business and can provide valuable insights into improvements and innovations.

DREAM SHAMELESSLY (AND OFTEN)

"You waste years by not being able to waste hours."
—Amos Tversky

Work is important. Staying on top of your inbox, keeping in touch with clients, and making sure you've always got money coming in are the foundations of productivity.

But they're not *everything*.

Sometimes, you need to step away from the desk and take a walk. Think about something you haven't thought about in twenty years. Do a little meditation. Write in a journal. Try to come up with an idea that you don't think would occur to anyone else, and don't be ashamed of the fact that you're "wasting time" by doing this.

People might laugh at you. They might ask why you're not glued to your desk making phone calls.

Don't listen.

Over the years, I've found that some of the best ideas I've ever had have come to me while I was sitting around "doing nothing." They've come in the brief moments when I pause to turn the page on the latest thriller novel that I'm reading, or while I'm tossing one of my kids into the pool in my backyard.

If you don't take a little time on occasion to daydream, you're going to miss out on some of your best ideas. This is especially true if you're doing creative work, which requires a certain degree of mental wandering for success. Most of the time, coming up with a creative solution involves seeing a given situation in ways that everyone else in the room didn't think of. That means you must do things that they weren't doing. Sometimes, that means going for an early morning run with no music to think about the problem, or buying a couple of tickets to a baseball game so you can think about things between innings.

Now, I'm aware that it might seem easy to say this when you're at my level, and you're *allowed* to take some time to think over your decisions. I'm aware that no one's going to wait for you, who might be working in cubicle eleven out in the bullpen, to come up with a creative solution to a problem while you do interpretive dance or something. But there are small ways that everyone can make their subconscious mind work for them.

Consider the case of Elias Howe, the inventor of the modern sewing machine. In 1845, Howe hit a wall in his work. He was trying to design a machine that could create a lockstitch—a stitch that would be secure enough to hold pieces of fabric together. Traditional hand sewing placed the eye of the needle—the hole where the thread passes—at the blunt end. Howe was certain that there was a way to make a machine do the job, but the specifics eluded him.

Frustrated and needing a break, Howe took a step back from his work. One night, he had a vivid dream of native warriors brandishing spears that had a hole near the spearhead. This vision provided the breakthrough he needed—he realized that he could place the eye of the needle at the pointed end, allowing the thread to loop correctly. The rest is history.

I'm sure anyone who's ever tried to write a song, a play, or a novel knows how important it can be to let the subconscious work for you. We all know about the Beatles, arguably the greatest band of all time. Paul McCartney, one of the principal songwriters, has frequently discussed how the tune for their iconic song "Yesterday" came to him in a dream.

McCartney woke up one morning with the melody fully formed in his mind. He didn't consciously sit and compose it; instead, it was the product of his subconscious mind at work while he slept. He initially thought he was recalling an existing song but soon realized that it was an original composition. And it wasn't just any song—it's one of the most covered songs in the history of recorded music.

The same thing happened to Keith Richards, the guitarist for the Rolling Stones, when he wrote the band's hit "Satisfaction." One day, he woke up with a tune in his head and picked up his guitar to try and figure it out.

What these anecdotes underline is a lesson that's often lost in the hustle and bustle of our modern work culture: your brain is still working even when you're not. Taking a step back from work, whether it's a brief break, a good night's sleep, or even a vacation, can allow your subconscious mind to break through the barriers your conscious mind has been banging its head against.

✒ Lesson 16

KEEP YOUR RELATIONSHIPS

"You will become like the five people you associate with the most. This can be either a blessing or a curse."

—Billy Cox

When I first met General John Kelly, I thought he was one of the toughest people I had ever met. In part, I believed this because that was the impression he sought to convey to the world. Whenever reporters wrote stories about him, they emphasized his love for order and his take-no-bullshit attitude. They pointed out that he'd been a fearsome Marine—one of the few men in our nation's history to rise through the ranks of that branch to earn the rank of four-star general. (Most people who attained that rank, I would later learn, came either from the Army or Navy.)

At the time, most people thought that a tough, take-no-bullshit asshole was exactly what our country needed. They were probably right. When Donald Trump shocked the world by winning the presidential election of 2016, the pickings for people to staff his White House were slim, to say the least. This is because most people who knew how to do the jobs that needed to be filled—

147

chief of staff, communications director, and all the smaller, less public-facing roles that really keep the executive branch running—didn't want to do those jobs under Trump. They had seen how the man had conducted himself during the campaign, and they sensed (quite rightly) that the man had no sense of loyalty. They knew that he would expect complete fealty from them but would reserve the right to fire and shame them in front of everyone at the slightest sign of trouble. If you read any book about the early years of the Trump White House—some of which are listed as suggested reading in the back of this book—you'll see the same pattern play out again and again. You'll also see people who would have gladly taken a job in the White House under Trump (or anyone, for that matter) but couldn't because they'd made negative comments about Trump in the past. Given how insecure the guy was, that was a big problem. No one who hadn't always expressed complete fealty to him and in all places (note the religious language there) could get so much as a janitorial position in his White House.

So, we had a big problem. The people who knew what they were doing were, for the most part, kept out of the White House, which was filled with bitter, insecure sycophants who'd tell Donald Trump everything he wanted to hear (mostly that he was very tall, very handsome, and right about everything all the time). That might have been great for Trump, who didn't seem focused on doing all that much work at the time, but it was bad for the American people.

General John Kelly, much as I might not have liked him personally then, was supposed to fix that. He was brought into the Trump White House, according to the many media reports that were written about him, to instill a sense of order.

Back then, of course, I believed that his hard-ass approach to the job was going to do more harm than good. I had been running companies for a few years by the time I got into politics, and I had always found that a fear-based approach to leadership didn't work. I hope you've been able to tell that from the advice I've given so far in this book.

That impression didn't change when I stepped through the doors of the building for the first time. From what I could tell, General Kelly—who'd arrived not long before I did—was looking to scare people into submission, and I didn't think that was going to pay off for him in the long run. What I didn't know at the time, of course, was just how bad the scale of the problem he was facing really was. Even as I watched Trump up close, I couldn't comprehend the sheer scale of the chaos this guy wanted to unleash on the United States. I certainly didn't know he was burning classified documents in the fireplace, as has been reported by the great Maggie Haberman in her book *Confidence Man*.

Then he fired me, which *really* made me sour on the guy. Even though he let me go in a way that was respectful and dignified—to the extent that dignity was possible at the time, given the outrageous circumstances—I still harbored a grudge, believing that if he really wanted to, he could have kept me on and allowed me to rehabilitate my reputation from the inside for a little while longer. Sure, I had cursed out a reporter and gravely insulted a few of the people I was working with (who deserved it, by the way), but in my mind, the situation was salvageable.

I was wrong, of course. But the mind operates in strange ways when it's desperate.

Now, the reason I'm telling you this story (again) isn't to take a few more shots at the fattest president in our nation's history. It's not to set myself up, once again, to crack a few jokes at the expense of the Diet-Coke-swilling, spray-tan-having, big dumb blob of a human being who occupied the Oval Office between 2017 and 2021. That would be immature.

I'm telling this story again because I want to talk about General John Kelly, who, much to my surprise, has become a close friend of mine in recent years. To this day, I can remember the moment when I realized that even after all I'd read about Kelly—and the *dozens* of minutes I'd spent talking to him during my eleven days in the White House—it still felt like I didn't really know the guy.

At the time, I knew the broad outline of his story. I knew that he was one of very few Marines to become a four-star general, and that he'd lost a son in combat. To me, that was the sum of Kelly— two facts gleaned from newspaper reports, and then the fact that he'd fired me (and didn't seem to like me very much).

Knowing that much, I could have grown resentful of the man. That, in fact, was my natural inclination, as it usually is when someone fires you. It makes sense, doesn't it? If you've ever had the misfortune of being fired from a job, I'm sure you can remember what it was like walking down the street with a box full of your things, silently having arguments in your head with the person who made the decision to let you go. You start to minimize their accomplishments to make yourself feel better, to come up with a version of that person in your head who's stupid, doesn't know anything, and only fired you to ruin your life because they're an asshole.

I used to be like that. But since I've been on the other side of the desk—I've had to fire dozens of people over the course of my career, usually under horrible circumstances—I can tell you that it's never a decision you come to lightly. Although it sounds like a cliché and is without a doubt the last thing a person who's being fired wants to hear, the line that's often said during these meetings really is true: It is, in fact, just as hard, if not harder, to be on the firing side of the desk.

That's why the person doing the firing almost always agonizes over the decision for months, wondering if there's some kind of program the person being fired can be put on to improve their performance. That's why there are countless meetings with HR and other departments to see if there's a way to avoid it. On the rare occasions that I've decided someone has to get fired, I've usually lost sleep about it the night before—and I'm not usually a guy who loses sleep over my decisions.

Sometimes, I lose sleep because it was *my* idea to hire the person whom I now have to let go. That means that in addition to the guilt I feel for taking away someone's livelihood and confidence—which is exactly what getting fired does to a person—I also have to take a hard look at my own decisions and see why I screwed up so bad. I should add here that when I decide to fire someone, it's almost never because that person is stupid or lazy. I pride myself on the fact that stupid or lazy people don't even make it through the door when it comes time to interview. Almost always, people get fired from SkyBridge, or my other ventures, because they're the wrong fit for the job they got—and that's on me, the person who gave them the position, much more than it is on them.

Now, I knew all this by the time John Kelly fired me. I had already hired and fired enough people to field two NFL football teams by the time I became the most famous fired guy in the country. But it took a few days before I could take the lessons I had learned about other people and really apply them to my situation.

So, I decided to read up on Kelly—to reject the urge to put the guy in the back of my mind, or to go on television and disparage

151

him to please the anti-Trump base and the CNN hosts who would have eaten up that kind of talk.

Slowly, as I read articles about his life and learned more about the conflicts that had made him into the person he is today, I realized he was not only a good guy, but a great one. To this day, I think General John Kelly is one of the finest Americans in this country, and that we'd be much better off if more people, especially young people, studied his life and learned from his example.

After a few years, I grew comfortable enough to call General Kelly on the phone. At first, these calls were just social. I wanted to bury the hatchet, sure, but I also wanted to reach out and see how he was doing. In the time that I'd spent reading up on him and getting back to my own business in New York City, General Kelly had also been fired by Donald Trump, who had come to loathe the notion that people thought Kelly was somehow more in charge of the White House than he was (which, of course, was the absolute truth).

After a few brief phone conversations with General Kelly, I had an idea. For the past fourteen years, I had been doing my annual SALT conference, the inception of which was discussed in the prologue to this book. In the beginning, this conference functioned in the way most conferences in the financial sector do. It was a way for people in my industry to meet one another, exchange ideas, and have a good time. But over the years, I had added another (somewhat selfish) element to the equation, which was the interviews I got to conduct with people I had admired my whole life.

As many of you may know, it's not easy to sit down and have a deep, hour-long conversation with people you admire. Most of the time, when you do get to meet these people, you're at a party or an event, and you speak for a few minutes at the most. You talk about your kids, your jobs, and wish one another well. There's no time to ask how they became the person they became, or to ask what advice they'd give people who want to do the same thing they do.

The longform interview, which is a format I've loved since I saw Dick Cavett, is a chance to ask those deep questions, and to give the person sitting across from you a chance to really think out their responses. When people have microphones in front of their faces—as anyone who's listened to a nice longform podcast lately can tell you—they can often feel more comfortable saying things that they wouldn't say otherwise. They'll tell you things that might seem self-indulgent or pretentious if you said them in casual conversation, and often those are the things that people respond to the most.

When I interviewed Caitlyn Jenner at the SALT conference several years ago, she explained with great honesty, tenderness, and compassion how the young Bruce always felt like a woman to the point where he thought he could run his way and work his way athletically, to becoming a man. Thus, he went on to win the 1976 gold medal for the decathlon, which he described as an overexaggerating over manliness. And yet despite that, she was a woman, and eventually relented to make the transition to her true identity.

To me, General John Kelly seemed like the perfect guy to go next in that lineup.

So, I gave him a call. By this point, we'd spoken a few times already, so it wasn't terribly weird for me to be asking. But there was still a very real sense that he might say no.

But he said yes. Not long after that phone call, General Kelly and I sat down in front of a packed crowd in Las Vegas and hashed out what had happened between us. We'd already done this to some degree in private, but it was nice to get things out in the open in front of a live audience.

Since then, we've become close, personal friends, and we often tour the country together to have conversations in front of people about work, leadership, and life in general. I always start these conversations by reminding the general that no matter how tough my questions get, he can't fire me again.

During our time speaking in front of audiences, General Kelly and I have gone well beyond politics. We've spoken about how to run an effective organization, how to stay connected to old friends, and how to keep your focus on family—which is what counts more than anything.

A few years ago, if you'd have told me that General Kelly and I would someday be performing in front of crowds all over the country, I would have assumed you were talking about some kind of C-list celebrity boxing tour. But reality has proven to be much better than that.

All because I swallowed my pride, kept the relationship, and reached out.

I am grateful to John Kelly for opening his heart to our friendship after all the initial soreness. He is a great patriot.

This week, try reaching out to three people you haven't talked to in a few months—or even a few years. The stories I've told in this lesson so far have all been about former bosses, but that doesn't mean your people have to be former bosses. It could be former colleagues, friends from college, or even former employees. Don't reach out with an agenda, and don't try to sell anyone anything. That'll make it seem like you're only calling because you read a book of advice from a hedge fund guy, and you think this person can advance your career.

This ties into something else we've talked about, which is that sometimes, you have to give up control a little. Don't be so intentional about every move that you make in your career. Let things happen—dream shamelessly—and you'll be amazed at what you can achieve, especially when you're not trying.

In other words: I'm not telling you to keep your relationships with people because it's going to get you a good job someday or because you're going to achieve great things with them.

I'm telling you to do it because the more people in your life, the better your life gets.

Like most true things, it really is that simple.

TREAT EVERYONE LIKE THEY'RE THE MOST IMPORTANT PERSON IN THE ROOM...BECAUSE THEY MIGHT BE

What follows is a short story.

But it's an enlightening one, so pay attention.

A few years ago, I was trying to raise money for a new fund I was starting. Given that I was entertaining some "high-net-worth individuals," as we say in the business, I would take them to a nice club on the east side of Manhattan. During lunches at this club, I would watch people talk down to the wait staff and ignore people who were supposedly below their station.

Nothing pisses me off more than that.

Now, it doesn't piss me off because I think I'm some ultra-kind man of the people (although I like to think that I'm pretty nice). It pisses me off because I've worked those bottom-of-the-ladder jobs, and I know what it's like to be stomped on by rich guys in dumb outfits.

But also...*you never know.*

Exhibit A: Every time I walked into this particular club for lunch, I would have the same waiter. I would always tip him well, and after a while we got to talking. After a few weeks, he knew what I did, and I knew a few things about where he had come from. One day, after a lunch that had gotten me nowhere, money-wise, this waiter mentioned to me that a relative had just died, and that he had come into an amount of money that was...shall we say, *eye-popping*, even for me.

I had this young man sit down, gave him some basic advice about money, and offered my services.

Today, his money is still with my fund, and he's done pretty well for himself. So have I.

The point? Treat everyone like they are the most important person in the room. Aside from being a nice guy, it might work out in your favor.

≋ Lesson 18

BE FEARLESS

"He who is not every day conquering some
fear has not learned the secret of life."

—RALPH WALDO EMERSON

I've had a lot of holy-shit moments in my life. Getting fired in front of millions of people was a big one. So was being lowered into deep water while strapped into a Jeep, then being told I had to sit there without moving for about ninety seconds while a camera crew filmed the whole thing.

Oh, and getting *literally* lit on fire (like, with a military-grade flamethrower) on television wasn't terribly pleasant either.

To this day, though, I still remember looking down at my phone around midnight on a Saturday in August of 2017 to find that I was now a character on *Saturday Night Live*.

Now, I did kind of expect this. In those days, taking a job in the White House—especially a public-facing one—all but guaranteed that you were going to get ripped apart on the news and late-night comedy programs. I wouldn't have been surprised to turn on the television and find that the guy who emptied the trash in the Oval Office was now a character on *SNL*. There was even a mocking analysis somewhere that suggested that our nation's comedians lost an estimated $4.1 billion because of my departure.

However, no matter how much you prepare yourself or imagine it in your head, there's really nothing that can prepare you to see some guy dressed as you, doing an impression of you, and saying grossly offensive things to make you look like an idiot on national television. *Saturday Night Live* might not have had the viewership numbers by the late 2010s that it did when I was a kid, but it was still a cultural institution. You couldn't even log onto the website of the *New York Times* on Sunday morning back then without seeing a full recap of everyone who'd been mocked and all the jokes that had been made the previous evening.

At first, I thought Bill Hader did a pretty good job with me. I thought the pinky ring he wore was funny, and that he talked with his hands just the right amount. I'm not sure he quite nailed the color of the dye I use in my hair, though, which is a shade I like to call "Latin American Dictator Brown." But you can't expect the hair and makeup people at *SNL* to nail *everything*.

Did I love the fact that he made me out to be some mentally challenged Italian meatball? No. I also wasn't too excited to see that Bill Hader seemed to be leaning on some of the oldest, laziest stereotypes about Italian Americans in the book. In his portrayal, I was loud, dumb, and probably connected to organized crime. When you said my last name three times, I showed up like some kind of "goombah Beetlejuice."

If I'm being completely honest—and, as we've already discussed, there's no good reason to be anything else—the portrayal did sting a little.

I'm sure my dramatic reaction to the sketch is due, at least in part, to the fact that I've been trying to dispute the notion that I'm just some dumb meathead for most of my life. I still remember what it was like to show up on the campus of Tufts University in Boston wearing my Gitano jeans, thinking I was hot shit, and being told that I looked like a total clown. I remember moments when I felt like I had to hide my heritage and who I was to please other people, or to stop talking the way I naturally talked because people were going to look down on me for it.

For whatever reason, the comedians are allowed to go after Italian tropes and stereotypes without any admonition or any public outcry. You can't call a Black person a pimp or a Jewish person a shylock, but you can call an Italian person a mafioso don. You can do that all day, with no problem in our society. The hypocrisy of that does bother people, but it does not bother me. I think we have too much sensitivity in our society. I'm a big believer in free speech, and a big believer in comedy.

Yet the hypocrisy *is* there.

When you make a decision to be a public figure, you have now created the space for people to viciously attack you, and to make fun of you if and when necessary, from a comedic perspective. To put it another way, if you decided to enter an NFL football game and step onto the field, unless you're a place kicker or a punter, it is guaranteed that you're going to get a concussion. You can't step into the White House Brady Press Briefing Room and speak to forty million people worldwide and not expect to be viciously attacked. It's called putting on your big boy pants.

When Bill Hader impersonated me on *Saturday Night Live*, I know this sounds bizarre, but I enjoyed it. I thought it was funny. Ironically, about a week later, I was sitting in the legend seats at a Yankee-Mets game at Yankee Stadium, next to Lorne Michaels, the creator of *Saturday Night Live*, and his friend Paul Simon, the legendary singer. Colin Jost, who is the anchor on the Weekend Update sketch segment, was also with them. Lorne turned to me, and said, "How did you feel about our rendition of you?"

I looked at him and smiled, and said I thought Bill could have used a little more hairspray, slightly more hair dye, and frankly, I didn't like the way he was tying his tie. All three of them laughed, and Lorne then invited me and my family to sit in the audience for that season's Christmas show.

On that show, Alec Baldwin, playing Donald Trump, was handed ornaments for a Christmas tree of love (which was all Ivanka ornaments, LOL). And my face, alongside Chris Christie and Jeff Sessions, adorned ornaments on the Christmas Tree of Hate, to the great delight of the studio audience. Of course, my family and I were laughing alongside them.

Why am I telling you this?

Because I've found that if you take the time and get to know anyone—even people who've wronged you, whom you think you're going to hate forever—you'll find that they're good people, just like you and your friends. You'll probably find that they do work you like, and that you can learn a great deal from them. Holding onto anger, like most stupid things we do, really comes from a place of fear and insecurity.

If you take yourself less seriously, you will find ironically that this is quite endearing to people.

Coming out and admitting you were wrong—or that someone's joke about you was pretty funny—is a small example of how you can show fearlessness. Don't be afraid to look stupid, and don't be afraid to admit that you were wrong about someone. Keep doing the things that make you feel alive, and don't let fear drive your decisions.

That doesn't mean you're not going to feel fear. It just means that you need to learn to control fear and make it work for you.

You know who's got some great advice on how to do this?

Bill Hader.

During several interviews after he left *SNL*, Hader admitted that he was deathly afraid every time he was about to go onstage. The fear got so bad that he started having panic attacks.

Then, one night, he was standing backstage next to the actor Jeff Bridges, who had been in dozens of great films by the time he showed up on the set of *Saturday Night Live*. As Hader tells it, they were about to perform a sketch together in which Hader played Julian Assange. He recalls how the fear came back in waves. *If I mess this up at all*, he thought, *the whole studio is going to fall down on me*.

That's a common fear, as anyone who's dealt with anxiety knows. Not only are you afraid you're going to screw up and embarrass yourself, but also you're afraid that the worst possible thing you can think of is going to happen, along with ten more bad things you haven't even thought of yet.

A few minutes before he was set to go on, Hader had a panic attack.

As he was recovering, Bridges came up to him and told him a story.

"I used to work with Robert Ryan," he said. "The great actor Robert Ryan. He said that before every take, he would start sweating. I said, 'Really? After all these years you still get nervous?' And he said, 'Oh, yeah. I would be really afraid if I wasn't afraid.'"

The point Jeff Bridges was trying to convey—which is an excellent one—is that when you care about your work, you're always going to feel a little afraid. That's a good thing. As Bridges told Hader just after he finished recounting that story, the anxiety you feel before you do something is an asset. Or, as he put it, "That's your buddy, man! Put your arm around it and bring it out there!"

If you've seen *The Big Lebowski*, I'm sure you're reading those last two lines in Jeff Bridges's voice. Good. Maybe that'll help you remember.

Because I think that advice is something we can all use.

Said another way: being fearless is not about making yourself free of fear; it's about learning how to use fear to your advantage.

Almost anyone who's succeeded during tough times has had the ability to do just that.

I don't think a lesson about fearlessness would be complete without telling a story about Winston Churchill, one of the most admirably fearless people who's ever walked the earth.

If you know anything about Churchill, it's probably that he was the prime minister of Great Britain who faced down the Nazis during World War II. You might also know that he had a curious way of dressing—always with a top hat and a cane, not to mention the big, fat cigars that hung from his mouth more or less all the time—and that he did a great deal of his business from the bathtub, often while sipping various kinds of alcohol (which he drank constantly throughout the day).

But even with all the pages of biography that have been written about Winston Churchill, a man who ranks just behind Jesus and Abe Lincoln for the most written-about people of all time, I still don't think most people understand how much courage he displayed in his life, or how many lessons we can learn simply by looking at how he acted during the most trying moments of his political career.

Taking the helm as prime minister in 1940, Churchill found Britain practically standing alone. The Nazis were on the march all over Europe, and it looked like they were coming for Britain next. Hard as it might be to imagine today, citizens of London had to walk to work every morning knowing that bombs might fall on their head. Considering the circumstances, it would have been easy to back down.

But as you may know, that's not what Winston Churchill did. Rather than compromising or negotiating with Hitler as many people wanted him to, he gave fiery, inspiring speeches to rally the nation. In one of the most famous, he promised that the people of Britain would "fight on the beaches...fight on the landing grounds...fight in the fields and in the streets," adding that they would "never surrender."

Even as the bombs were falling, Churchill told the people of Britain to go about their business, and to keep a stiff upper lip in the face of adversity.

Of course, that doesn't mean he wasn't afraid. As several biographers have pointed out in the years since, Churchill was all too aware of the gravity of the situation, perhaps more than anyone else. His fearlessness was his conscious choice to meet these fears head-on, to tackle rather than retreat. As he once put it, "Fear is a reaction. Courage is a decision."

His fearless demeanor during the war, his refusal to surrender in the face of adversity, exemplified this sentiment, inspiring Britain and ultimately leading them to victory. His fearlessness during World War II remains an enduring testament to his character, shaping his legacy as one of history's greatest leaders.

➤ ➤ ➤

Fearlessness, as we've seen, is one of the toughest of all traits to truly develop. We are raised to always have it. We fear authority and are coerced early to take direction, to conform and fit in. Failure causes fear. Fear creates the self-talk of caution and complacency. Fear also chants to us that we aren't enough. Good enough. It is for others but not for us.

We can never truly become completely fearless. We wouldn't *want* to become completely fearless either.

The point, as we've seen over the last few pages, is not to live without fear. It's to recognize that fear is a good sign. It means we're still in the game, and we still care deeply about what we're doing. When you're afraid of failing at something, it's because you care about doing it well.

So, don't be afraid to be afraid. But don't ever let fear stop you from doing what you know is right.

HAVE PERSPECTIVE

If you've listened to me talk—not to mention read the preceding hundred pages or so—you probably know that I can be a little colorful with my language sometimes. Over the course of my career, I've found that being authentic to myself, which means cursing every once in a while and making the occasional off-color joke, is better than trying to conform to someone else's idea of how I should act.

So, I haven't always had the easiest time telling my kids not to swear. It's a real "do as I say, not as I do" issue in the Scaramucci household.

But there have always been two words that I won't let my children say in my presence—or anyone's presence, for that matter.

Those words are "should" and "ought."

Let me explain.

We live in a reality-based society, not a normative one. So, although we can expect fairness all we want, it's never going to happen. Even when we do everything right—when we're nice to all the right people, we give to all the right charities, and we don't use any curse words—things can still go sideways on us, often through no fault of our own.

Is that the way things *should* be? Probably not. But it's the way things are.

Should the government borrow forty-nine cents of every dollar they are spending? No. But they do. Should a guy who told a bunch of lunatics to storm the Capitol building because he couldn't handle the fact that he got his ass kicked in the presidential election be running for president again? No!

But it's happening.

In other words, bad things happen to good people for no reason. Even if we think we ought to get into the college of our dreams, it doesn't happen. Even when we think that a business we've built ought to go to the moon, it doesn't.

Like many of the serious problems we face, this one isn't new. Some of the best thinkers in the history of Western civilization have been dealing with it for centuries.

Marcus Aurelius, the stoic Roman emperor, once said, "Very little is needed to make a happy life; it is all within yourself, in your way of thinking." His wisdom underscores the power of perspective. If we cultivate a lens of gratitude and awareness, we begin to see the richness in our lives. We see the privilege in the mundane, the extraordinary in the ordinary.

Take the example of Helen Keller, who despite being blind and deaf, became an influential author, political activist, and lecturer. She once said, "I cried because I had no shoes until I met a man who had no feet." Keller's perspective transformed her life. She didn't let her physical disabilities limit her but instead used them as a catalyst to enrich her life and the lives of others.

How, then, can we cultivate this perspective? Firstly, by practicing gratitude. Take a few moments each day to reflect on what you're thankful for. It could be as simple as a hot cup of coffee, a heartwarming conversation with a friend, or a peaceful walk in the park. This daily practice shifts our focus from lack to abundance and nurtures a positive outlook.

Secondly, expand your horizons. Travel, read, and interact with diverse people. Learn about different cultures, histories, and ways of life. As you expose yourself to the diversity of human experiences, your understanding deepens, your empathy broadens, and your perspective shifts. You begin to see your own life in a new light, appreciating your privileges and opportunities.

Finally, use your abundance to make a difference. Kindness is a powerful agent of perspective. In reaching out to others, in lending a helping hand, we not only make a tangible difference in someone's life but also gain a deep appreciation for our blessings.

In conclusion, cultivating a perspective of gratitude and awareness doesn't mean ignoring life's challenges or brushing aside personal struggles. It simply means acknowledging the goodness that already exists in our lives, even amid adversity. It means recognizing our privileges and using them to make a difference. After all, it is perspective that turns the sun into a "yellow star" or a "warm sphere of splendor." Your life—and the world—is what you choose to see.

Just taking the reality-based approach, we can gain a healthy perspective, one of no entitlement so that we bump up on every glimmer of positivity. When we see with great gratitude, joy, and appreciation, the entire world changes for us. Want to survive a crisis? Have perspective. It fits for everything in any scenario.

❧ Lesson 20

BE "TOUGHNICE"

"Play nice, but win."

—Michael Dell

So, I'm inventing a word. Sue me.

The thing is, I've always had trouble articulating my management style. Usually, when I'm asked how I run my company, I say that the most important thing I do is empower people. If you're in my office, it means I trust you. If you have an idea, run with it. If you think you know better than I do, don't listen to me. I'm not going to be looking over your shoulder and checking up on your progress, making my little edits and suggestions while you're trying to get your work done.

This has helped me, for the most part, but I have also trusted and empowered people who have hurt me. I do believe, however, that the totality of this management philosophy has enabled me to do more and accomplish more because of my willingness to delegate and to empower people.

But when that work hits my desk, it had better be good. I'm not going to sugarcoat my criticisms if I think you've screwed up royally.

So, *toughnice.*

When things get tough, *you* have to get tough. But you also have to be nice.

See how I got there?

Now, a few caveats. I'm not saying that you should be nice one minute and ultra-tough the next. You're not a Sour Patch Kid. Changing up your style minute to minute like that can make people feel unsafe around you. It can make them feel like they don't know how to please you, and all of a sudden, they're walking on eggshells because they don't know how you're going to react. They'll start to wonder: *Am I walking into the nice guy's office? Or the tough guy's?*

Instead, you must blend these two modes of operating into one. That's why I smashed them together into one word. And sure, I don't think the term is genius or anything. It's definitely not going to be in the next packet of Harvard Business School case studies that professors use to analyze good management style.

But it is important if you're going to be managing people. At its core, "toughnice" is a feeling where people recognize that they are willing make tough decisions and willing to be tough on others that are being unfair. People want to feel like you're a tough guy, but that you'll be tough *on their behalf* when the going gets tough.

BE RESILIENT

When I first started making notes for the book you are reading—or the book you're skimming through, if that's your thing—one of the first things that came to me was a title.

That title, which I typed out with a sense of glee that I haven't experienced since I was very young, was:

F@#K ME? NO, F@#K YOU!

Ten Skills to Keep You in the Game

Even though I host a weekly podcast about books, I tend to stick more to the content of those books and the opinions of people who write them, rather than the business side of things. So, I was genuinely surprised when I started getting feedback from agents, editors, and fellow authors that a book with two f-bombs in the title was probably not going to sell a whole lot of copies. Other than Amazon, which sells just about everything you can think of, almost no reputable establishment in the country would have carried the book if I'd gone with my original instincts.

So, I came up with another title. I also added a few more lessons, which came to me as I reviewed the story of my life and all that I've been able to learn along the way.

But there's an old saying about creative work that goes something like: *first thought, best thought.* Although I haven't always found that to be the case, there's definitely some truth to it. Often, the first thing that pops into your head when you sit down to do creative work is the thing that's most integral to whatever you're trying to create. Sometimes, you don't even know why it's in your head until you've written a few hundred pages, which is exactly what happened with my title.

At this point in the book, I've come to realize that the single most important skill you can cultivate in life—and therefore the most important lesson in this book—is resilience. This is the most important skill because without it, everything else is useless. There's no point in being disciplined, for instance, if you're going to curl up in a ball and cry every time something bad happens to you. There's no reason to have good ideas, or to build good relationships in the way that I've suggested so far, if you can't push past the bad things in life.

In some sense, we've already touched on the need for resilience. In Lesson 12, we talked about how to push through creative blocks, and how to keep pushing even when you don't like the work you're doing. At its core, finishing what you start is all about building resilience: it allows you to repeat the process of doing the work (even when you might not like it) and fixing whatever you did until you're happy with it.

But resilience is also important on a large scale. It's especially important when dealing with other people, and the outside world in general.

As I'm sure you know, other people can be tough. This is especially true if you're in the public eye, or even if you're doing work that's going to be judged by your peers. Sometimes, the people in your own community can be your toughest critics. I know that when I slip up, my harshest critics are usually other businessmen and financial journalists who've been keeping track of my career for years. Oddly enough, it's their criticism that stings the most because they know me best.

The same is true in most fields. When a physicist publishes a new paper on the origins of the universe, for instance, there's no one who'll attack that scientist with more fervor—and more glee, usually—than other scientists who have similar theories. When you're working in a small community, all fighting for the attention of the outside world and limited resources (usually grant money), people have an interest in taking one another down.

So, no matter what field you're in, there are always going to be people who want to see you fail. The best among us, of course, won't do that. They'll realize that rising tides lift all boats, and that success for one person in a community usually begets success for everyone else. Sadly, though, the people who want you to fail will always have more power over you if you let them. They're the ones who will attack your products, write bad reviews of your book, and spread rumors about you.

If you've learned anything from the preceding pages, I hope that it's the importance of tuning out the bad voices and bouncing back from attacks of this nature. As I've said repeatedly—and will say as many times as I have to—you can't control the bad shit that happens to you, even if that bad stuff comes as a direct result of your decisions (such as deciding to hang around bad people). What you can control is how you respond. That, as Viktor Frankl tells us in *Man's Search for Meaning*, as well as in the rest of his excellent writings, is what makes a person.

So, a few words about resilience.

Like most things, you can learn it.

As with most things, keeping yourself in a "growth mindset" is important. This, as we discussed in the earlier lessons of this book, is the ability to see challenges as opportunities rather than as barriers. It's about looking at a problem and being able to ask what it can teach you rather than letting your brain run wild with negative scenarios. Learning to recognize when you're "catastrophizing," i.e., playing out all the worst things that can happen in your head repeatedly, is a good first step. If you fail to close a deal, for instance, don't let your brain go crazy and think that this is going to zap your confidence, that you're never going to close a deal again, and that you and your family are going to be living on the street in a set of cardboard boxes.

Instead, breathe. Ask yourself what went wrong while you were on the phone with the client. Did you make a joke that didn't go over well? Did you fail to recognize an opportunity to offer him a service that only you can provide? Asking yourself these questions and being able to learn from the answers is one of the most important things you can do to develop a growth mindset. This will allow you to transform difficult situations into stepping stones rather than brick walls that you smash into.

After that, it all goes back to Lesson 4, about having an optimistic mindset. As I said before, when you practice optimism daily, your worldview changes completely. You learn to see the best not only in other people, but in situations. Suddenly, that failure to finish your latest YouTube video—or whatever you've been working on—isn't proof that you're a loser and you never should have tried to become an online commentator in the first place. It's just further proof that you've got a lot to learn.

Put it this way. If you noticed that the work you did was bad, you're already about sixty percent of the way toward getting better. There are millions of people in the world who do bad work every day—bad writing, bad painting, and bad marketing—and leave the office or the studio at five o'clock genuinely believing what they did was good. When someone tells them that the work they did was bad, they have no idea what to do because they don't really know *why* it's bad.

But you do! So, look at the video you made, the chapter you wrote, or the PowerPoint deck you created and figure out what it is about the work that's making you feel like you want to puke. There's a pretty good chance that you've just failed to live up to the ideal version of the thing you set out to create in your head, in which case you should give it a light edit and show it to someone else.

But if you look long enough, you'll be able to be objective about what you've done wrong. Make a short list of those things and ask yourself what specific steps you can take to fix them. If you can identify what you've done wrong, you're more than halfway through the process of making it better.

This doesn't just apply to creative work. It applies to business as well. If you walk away from an interaction with a client with a big pit in your stomach, you're already better off than most people. Think about it. Some people say stupid things, walk away, and think they just did a great job. If you can be self-critical enough to realize when you've screwed up—but not so self-critical that you crumble into a ball and never want to leave the house again—you're already more resilient than most people on earth.

All you have to do is take your problems one at a time, break them up into small, actionable pieces, and work on fixing them. Again, this is all about mindfulness. Don't think about what's going to happen, and don't think too much about what already happen. Just stay in the moment, figure out how to solve the problems that are right in front of your face, and keep charging ahead.

Are you wondering whether I'm going to tell you another story about Winston Churchill?

Well, buckle up. Because I am.

Reading the story that I told you a few lessons ago, you might get the impression that Winston Churchill was a hero all his life. You might think that anyone who had such an uncanny ability to defy conventional wisdom the way he did, treating Adolf Hitler like the monster that he was when so many in Britain refused to do so, must have had an iron will from the moment he was born.

But he didn't. Much like Theodore Roosevelt, who built himself up physically after a childhood spent mostly in bed and his father's arms, Churchill did not have an easy road to the position he'd eventually come to occupy.

For many years, he failed far more than he succeeded. Born to upper class parents in 1874, the young Churchill struggled in school, earning terrible grades on his exams. He had to apply to military college three times before they let him in. Even then, he didn't do well in his classes, and chose the cavalry that demanded less from recruits academically.

Although he read a great deal on his own, he hated school. His biographer Andrew Roberts, who published a book in 2018 called *Churchill: Walking with Destiny*, called Churchill "one of the greatest individualists of modern times."

But his rigid individuality didn't help him during the Second Boer War, which brought Churchill to South Africa as a soldier. He also wrote part-time for various newspapers back home. While in South Africa, he was captured by the enemy and held in a prison camp for many months.

Although this is a small, and relatively minor, part of Churchill's biography now, I'm sure it seemed huge at the time—especially for Churchill, who was the one locked up in a foreign country. If you'd lived that guy's life, failing constantly at everything you tried, always seeming to fall back to the middle of the pack despite the high station you were born into, you might have gotten discouraged as well.

But Churchill escaped, returning to his home country a hero. Rather than wallowing in the shame of having been captured, he drew on his experiences in South Africa to write a book about what had happened to him. Mere months after his return, that book became a bestseller and made Churchill a minor celebrity.

On the strength of his writing, he was elected to a seat in the House of Commons at the age of twenty-six. Once he'd done that job for a few years—overseeing different projects for the British empire, mostly to do with its far-flung colonies—he became First Lord of the Admiralty.

Amazingly, this is when the real failure began, and the need for resilience became dire. In February of 1915, Churchill led a group of men into the Dardanelles straits near modern-day Istanbul. Their mission was to retake the land from the Ottoman Empire, which had held it for more than six hundred years.

After a short battle, they failed, and 214,000 soldiers died. Many people in the British government blamed Churchill for the failure, and he resigned from government entirely over the matter.

A few years later, he joined the army as an enlisted man, traveling to the trenches in Belgium. While serving in those miserable conditions, he was nearly killed many times.

Even after all that—the kind of failure that would cripple most men, combined with a miserable three years in some of the worst conditions soldiers have ever had to endure—Churchill continued to serve his country. In the decade that he was out of government, he read widely and wrote many books and articles about history. He warned often of the threat that Hitler posed to the world, even as many of his former colleagues urged Neville Chamberlain, the prime minister, to negotiate with him.

It was around this time that Churchill wrote the line that opens this chapter, that "success is the ability to go from failure to failure without losing enthusiasm."

Luckily for the world, he didn't lose enthusiasm, despite having fallen from grace several times over.

When Germany invaded Czechoslovakia in 1939, the British government realized that they needed someone who was willing to fight like hell against the Nazis. So they re-appointed Churchill as First Lord of the Admiralty. Not long after, when it became clear that Chamberlain had underestimated Hitler, King George VI asked Churchill to become prime minister.

When we tell stories about Winston Churchill's bravery today— which I did just a few pages ago—we don't often think about how many seemingly catastrophic failures the man had to endure on his way back to the top of the British government. We don't think about the time he spent in prison, the guilt he must have felt after allowing 214,000 of his own men to die, or the grave doubts that must have crept into his mind at every stage of his life.

But we should.

We should also be mindful of how Churchill endured those setbacks. You'll notice that after every major failure in his life, Churchill returned to the things that he'd loved since he was a kid—the things that brought him joy and allowed him to express himself: reading and writing about history. Oddly enough, it was that reading and writing that convinced him of what no one else could see: that Hitler was a monster, and that the man could not be reasoned with.

If you've never read a biography of Churchill, I'd strongly recommend Andrew Roberts's *Churchill: Walking with Destiny*. As you read it, pay attention to all the amazing ways that one man was able to overcome failure to do great things. More importantly, see how you might do the same in your own life.

Unless you've made some *very* bad decisions, you're not dealing with something as bad as allowing more than two hundred thousand men under your command to die. But you might feel like it. As the old saying goes, the worst thing that ever happened to you is the worst thing that ever happened to you. When you're going through tough times, being told there are people who've been through worse and come out the other side doesn't help all that much.

Except that sometimes it does. When I was going through my own rough patch of road, it helped me immensely to read the words of people who'd gone through similar things before me. Maybe that's why in the pages of this book, I've reached so often for quotes from Viktor Frankl, Winston Churchill, and Teddy Roosevelt, all of whom endured great failure on their way to success. If these men had anything in common, it was that they never believed their best days were behind them.

And you shouldn't either.

Speaking of Teddy Roosevelt, here's a quote that I've always loved from one of his most famous speeches, delivered at the Sorbonne in Paris in April of 1910. This speech, known today as the "Man in the Arena" address, was called Citizenship in a Republic at the time it was delivered.

Reading it today, you can see why the "man in the arena" quote has come to replace the original title. Consider what it must have been like, sitting there in the audience as a Frenchman (or French lady) at the turn of the twentieth century and hearing the great man deliver this for the first time:

> It is not the critic who counts; not the man who points out how the strong man stumbles, or where the doer of deeds could have done them better. The credit belongs to the man who is actually in the arena, whose face is marred by dust and sweat and blood; who strives valiantly; who errs, who comes short again and again, because there is no effort without error and shortcoming; but who does actually strive to do the deeds; who knows the great enthusiasms, the great devotions; who spends himself in a worthy cause; who at the best knows in the end the triumph of high achievement, and who at the worst, if he fails, at least fails while daring greatly, so that his place shall never be with those cold and timid souls who neither know victory nor defeat. Shame on the man of cultivated taste who permits refinement to develop into fastidiousness that unfits him for doing the rough work of a workaday world. Among the free peoples who govern themselves there is but a small field of usefulness open for the men of cloistered life who shrink from contact with their fellows. Still less room is there for those who deride or slight what is done

by those who actually bear the brunt of the day; nor yet for those others who always profess that they would like to take action, if only the conditions of life were not exactly what they actually are. The man who does nothing cuts the same sordid figure in the pages of history, whether he be cynic, or fop, or voluptuary. There is little use for the being whose tepid soul knows nothing of the great and generous emotion, of the high pride, the stern belief, the lofty enthusiasm, of the men who quell the storm and ride the thunder. Well for these men if they succeed; well also, though not so well, if they fail, given only that they have nobly ventured, and have put forth all their heart and strength.

Again, that's enough to make me want to ride into battle behind the guy. I wouldn't have even asked where we were going first.

But it also underscores a key point, which is that critics don't matter. The people who want you to fail will always want you to fail. The only thing you can do is stay in the arena and keep fighting. Eventually, the critics will come around.

And if they don't?

Well, fuck them.

And who knows? You might inspire others. Roosevelt and Churchill certainly did. In fact, Winston Churchill, according to the biographer Erik Larson, who wrote a great book about the Blitz titled *The Splendid and the Vile*, notes that in addition to everything else that was admirable about the guy, Churchill also had a "striking trait: his knack for making people feel loftier, stronger, and, above all, more courageous."

That is why so many people remember the man's name. And that is what you should strive for in any position of leadership. Don't worry about making people think that you're strong, courageous, or competent. Focus on making *other* people feel that way. Not only is that a good thing to do for moral reasons, it also assures that those people will have your back when things go south.

And take it from me. Sooner or later, things *are* going to go south. Prepare for it.

To this day, many people believe that this ability came from Churchill's vast knowledge of history, and his ability to choose exactly the right words to inspire people. But reading his biography, it's clear that it comes from somewhere much deeper. It is a skill that can only be developed by understanding what it's like to fail—not just once, but over and over again, so often that people seem to believe that failing is all you can do—and learning from that experience.

That is why resilience is so important—not only because it allows you to get better every day, but because it shows the people around you that failure does not have to be the end of the road.

Or, as Winston Churchill, who was a much better writer than I'll ever be, famously put it: "Success is not final, failure is not fatal: It is the courage to continue that counts."

In closing: No success happens without resilience. It is the number one factor. I know no entrepreneur, no genius, no Nobel Prize winner, not anyone who has accomplished anything that has been going through a downturn—a bad spell, a health problem, a death of a family member, a product failure, a disastrous relationship—somewhere in the chain of their life. The number one thing is to persevere, to ignore the naysayers, and to recognize that you're in the arena, putting up a great fight to be in love with the journey and less concerned about the destinations.

Once you commit to the concept of perseverance, it becomes a habit, and it's ingrained in your personality so that no matter what is happening, no matter how we perceive the badness of the catastrophe, it actually doesn't matter to your spirit or soul; you're committed and you're driving forward.

HAVE A HEALTHY MINDSET

Over the course of this book, I've given you a great deal of advice. I'm hoping that at least some of it was stuff you hadn't heard before.

But I'm sure that for the most part, you knew this stuff already. All I'm really doing here is confirming that everything that you've heard is good for you since you were a little kid—having discipline, finding joy, and giving back to your community—really *is* good for you. I can tell you this because I've been trying (and often failing) to find happiness my entire adult life.

Here's another truism that really is true:

Eating right and exercising really is good for you.

I know, I know. You were hoping that you could skate by on two half-assed gym sessions a month and dinners at the steakhouse every few days.

But you can't. Especially not as you get on in years.

I get why this kind of thing doesn't seem important. Today, most people don't have to do manual labor as part of their jobs—at least not the back-breaking kind that my relatives grew up doing (and some of my friends still do today). Most of us think that our minds are the most important things we have. They're what solve our problems at work, write our reports, and keep the money coming in. So, we assume that mental activities are more important than physical ones. We make excuses for why we can't go to the gym this week, and we put off those morning walks because we'd rather be at our desks crafting emails or meditating to prepare our minds for the day ahead.

But the mind and the body are linked.

As the Roman philosopher Seneca once said, "We treat the body rigorously so that it will not be disobedient to the mind."

Nice, right?

Deep down, we all know that there will come a day when our bodies are going to betray us. We're going to want to walk to a meeting, and we'll get winded by the time we've gone a few blocks. We'll get asked to play golf to talk through a deal, and we'll have to decline because we can't lift the clubs out of the trunk of our car.

Getting a little exercise—or doing anything extracurricular—will make sure that day is as far in the future as possible.

So, if you're lucky enough to have two legs that both work, get out there and use them. Go for a jog. Hop on a bicycle.

What you do isn't important. What *is* important is that you push yourself a little further every time you step outside to do your physical work. It doesn't matter if you're putting a little more weight on the bar every time you lay down to bench press or if you're shaving a few seconds off your mile time whenever you go for a run. Aim to be better than you were the day before.

The point of all these exercises isn't to turn you into an athlete in peak form or to help you lose weight (although that might happen along the way). The point, as any good athlete can tell you, is to show your body that your mind is in charge.

At some point during your exercises, especially if you haven't done them in a long time (or ever), you're going to feel like you want to quit. The first few times, you might give into that impulse. But the first time you don't—the first time you push through the rest of a mile even though you're running on fumes, or crank out a few more reps in the gym even though your arms are shaking—you'll get a feeling of accomplishment that's hard to get anywhere else.

Think about it. In your day-to-day life, you don't get many clear-cut examples of progress. When it comes to just about every skill you know—whether it be reading, math, or picking stocks—you probably stopped improving by leaps and bounds years ago. These days, your progress is so small that you don't often notice it. You don't get the rush of accomplishment anytime you do something good in your daily life anymore.

With exercise, you can get one every day. Whenever you finish a mile faster than you did the day before, you'll be able to see your own progress in cold, hard numbers. The same goes for weights in the gym or free throws in basketball.

Then, who knows. Sign up for a local race. Join a biking team.

It doesn't even have to be physical. Take up the guitar or the piano. Learn to sew or paint watercolors.

One of the most important parts about having a healthy mindset is getting away from the thing that you do all day and working on yourself in some other way.

Trust me. No one needs this advice more than I do. While I do manage to get to the gym most days, I don't have most of the traditional male hobbies. I don't golf. I don't like to camp out in the woods or go shooting. Most of my free time is spent with my children and my wife Deidre. But in a way, that can be its own kind of escape from the daily life.

The key is to figure out what *your* escape is and get good at it. Or don't get good at it. The point of having one of these escapes is that you don't have to be good at all. Just mess around, decompress, and relax.

It'll help you in the long run. I promise.

BE SECURE

"Alright, that's enough."

I was sitting near the front of Air Force One with President Donald Trump and a few of his close aides. It was July 25, 2017, my fifth day in the White House.

For the past few minutes, I had been listening to a smart, incredibly patient White House policy advisor explain the finer points of a peace treaty that had been signed between Israel and Palestine many years earlier.

Given that President Trump had promised to bring peace to the Middle East during his first term in office—something he believed would be pretty easy, not unlike picking out paint colors for a hotel hallway—the policy experts around him figured it would be good if he at least knew the broad history of the region, which would include a few details about this treaty. So, they'd sent along an expert to brief him on the plane, which was headed to a rally in Youngstown, Ohio.

It wasn't going well.

Although I had only worked in the White House a few days, I was beginning to pick up the tricks for getting through to President Trump. I had learned that if you wanted to get through to him on a topic that was even mildly complex, your best bet was to trap him in a confined space. Only then could you make sure that he wouldn't kick you out of the room as soon as he got bored, which usually happened quickly.

Even when you had him trapped, of course, you bounced up against the limits of the man's intellect, which wasn't exactly stellar. Most of the aides I knew found that using pictures was a good way to get him to follow along. So was using small words and referencing cultural touchstones with which he might be familiar—old films, for instance, or certain songs by Elton John. If you could figure out a way to relate the topic at hand to professional wrestling or reality television, that'd be ideal, too.

But as we all soon found out, the Israel-Palestine conflict doesn't exactly lend itself to light summary. You can't really understand what's going on in the region by using the SparkNotes, as we so often had to do when briefing Donald J. Trump.

So, after about two minutes, the foreign policy expert had hit a wall. Despite several attempts to keep President Trump's attention, he kept getting waved off. Finally, the president declared that he'd had enough, and started bullying the guy about his expertise in the subject. He talked about how smart he was, and how he was better than all the intellectuals who were always coming into the Oval Office to brief him on complex subjects. I felt like I was back in the hallway of my high school watching some bully getting ready to stuff a nerd into his locker. It was embarrassing.

So, I tried to step in and salvage the situation.

"Mr. President," I said, interrupting some tirade about television or the Democrats (I don't really remember). "Have you ever seen the movie *Lawrence of Arabia*?"

Suddenly, the president was engaged again. He turned in my direction, allowing the policy analyst to sink back in his chair and enjoy a brief respite from the verbal abuse he'd been suffering at the hands of his boss, who, amazingly, just so happened to be the president of the United States. President Trump said he remembered *Lawrence of Arabia* very well. And then he was off.

"Peter O'Toole was great in that. Such a great actor. Really terrific."

"He was," I said. "He was. Now, if you think about that movie, there was a conflict in the Middle East, and there was a treaty between the British and the French that was called the Sykes–Picot Agreement that purposefully drew the boundary lines of each of these countries in a way that would instigate tribal territorial disputes. Effectively, they created, because of that treaty, a permanent conflict in the Middle East. In some ways, Mr. President, we're still fighting and trying to resolve elements of the First World War."

Now, I'm sure that you find this story embarrassing. You should. Maybe it makes you angry to know that the guy who ran our country (sort of) for five years didn't know some very basic things about global affairs, and ruthlessly mocked anyone who tried to enlighten him. Maybe you find it strange that President Trump wouldn't just listen to his advisors, who are literally hired to tell him what he doesn't know.

I'm sure you know that throughout history, every president has had advisors. Even George Washington, who came into office having no idea what the American government should look like, made it a priority to hire the smartest people he could find. This is because Washington, in addition to being brave, smart, and honorable, was also *secure*. As an example, he had as his right-hand person Alexander Hamilton, who was arguably tied with Benjamin Franklin for being the most intellectually adept and versatile of the founding fathers. He knew that he didn't know everything, and he knew that he would need other people around him to fill the gaps in his knowledge.

In Washington's case, the humility was hard earned. One of his first major military operations resulted in the deaths of many hundreds of men, all of whom were under his command. For years, Washington carried guilt from that operation, as well as a knowledge that charging ahead without thinking was not always the best approach.

When you look through history, you realize that great men and women don't get where they are by trusting their gut all the time. Sure, there are times when these people do ignore everyone around them and make a risky call based on gut feeling alone. I've done that several times, including when I decided to put on the first SALT conference in Las Vegas during the worst years of the financial crisis over the advice of every single one of my partners. But those stories are extremely rare, and they often don't pan out. That's why we remember the rare times that they *do* work out. I also trusted Sam Bankman-Fried and look how badly that ended.

Even the best leaders need good people around them. The more responsibilities a leader has, the better the people that person needs around him or her. Sometimes, that means hiring your enemies. Sometimes, it means bringing in someone who's so smart they make you feel like the dumbest guy ever to live (which I've done several times). This is important. I like to say that A-players always hire A-players—people who are better than them in every conceivable way. B-players, on the other hand, hire people who aren't going to be a threat. They bring in other B-players, C-players, and people from the minor leagues, so they never have to feel threatened.

Look at the staff of the Trump White House—at least most of the inner circle—and you'll see exactly what I mean. The people who really knew what they were doing were often laughed out of the room in favor of yes-men and sycophants who'd tell President Trump exactly what he wanted to hear. Anyone who contradicted him, or talked to him straight, was quickly shown the door.

Even though I was only in the building for eleven days, I saw it happen several other times. One of them occurred a few days before the plane trip I described a few pages ago, when I attended another briefing with President Trump about the situation in the Middle East. This one was in the Oval Office.

That morning, for what seemed like the hundredth time, a group of subject-matter experts were attempting to explain to the man how complicated the issue of Israel and Palestine was. Many presidents, they said, had been attempting to reach some kind of peace agreement in the region for decades, usually finding themselves right back where they started. Even people who'd been studying the issue their whole lives seemed to realize that the issue was far more complicated than they'd once believed.

The same thing had happened to me, by the way. Despite all the years I had spent doing business in the Middle East by that point, I found that after just a few days of reading daily briefings in the White House, I knew less than I ever had before.

Of course, I actually read the things. I can't say the same for our forty-fifth president.

On the day in question, some poor guy was trying to explain to President Trump the difference between Shia Muslims and Sunni Muslims. Again, it was something that we all figured he should know, given that he'd promised to bring peace to the Middle East, where many of the world's billion and a half Muslims live. As soon as the meeting started and President Trump had been brought his obligatory Diet Coke (brought by a naval steward when the president pressed a special red button on the Resolute desk), the subject-matter expert started talking about the seventh century.

"It was then," he said, "that Muhammad, the founder of the Islamic faith, had died, leaving two warring factions in his wake. The first faction, known as Sunnis, believed that..."

...and that was about as far as we got.

"I'm done," President Trump said. "That's enough. Thank you."

We all looked stunned.

A few days after the meeting, speaking with Jared Kushner, I learned (as many aides had learned before me) that there was a very specific way you had to deal with President Trump—at least if you wanted him to understand a single thing you were saying. Small words were key, as were pictures. But most importantly, you could never, *ever*, make him feel dumb. As soon as you did that, he'd start to go at you. He'd bully you. He'd talk about how much money he had or how amazing it was that he'd won in 2016.

And before you knew it, the meeting would be over. The aides would all break up, and nothing would have gotten done.

Embarrassed? Shocked?

You should be.

Look, not knowing things sucks. I'll be the first to admit that.

My whole life, I've tried to read as much as possible, speak with as many people as possible, and pay attention the whole time so I can avoid not knowing things. And I *still* feel like the dumbest person in most rooms I walk into.

There are times when this is discouraging. Some days I look at the pile of books I haven't read yet and shake my head, knowing there are some I'll never be able to get to. Some nights I wake up in a cold sweat thinking that I made the wrong decision that day because I didn't have all the information, then I spend the rest of the night running through other scenarios in my mind.

Usually, what gets me back to sleep is knowing that I'm surrounded by very smart people, and that we've had a great deal of success together in the past. Tomorrow, I'll wake up and acquire more knowledge than I did the day before, and if I don't know something, I'll ask. Humility goes a long way toward making you feel secure in yourself, because it always reminds you that it's possible to get better.

You'll never know that you don't know something until you meet someone who *does* know that thing and they make you look stupid.

I mean, imagine the list of things you don't know. I'm willing to bet that unless you're a freaky genius—or you're part of a secret early test group for Elon Musk's Neuralink—that list is much longer than the list of things you do know. After a while, you realize that you don't even know what things to put on the list because you don't know them. I'm sure that unless you happen to be an expert in the subject, you don't know a whole lot about neuroscience or when the pyramids of Egypt were built.

And that's okay.

Acknowledging our ignorance may feel uncomfortable, even threatening. After all, we're taught to display confidence, to project an aura of competence. But in the quest for credibility, we often forget that no one, however experienced or talented, knows it all. And therein lies the irony: true credibility comes not from showcasing an all-encompassing knowledge, but from the courage to unveil our ignorance and the humility to learn.

Consider the philosophy of Socrates, one of the greatest thinkers of all time. His method of inquiry, the Socratic method, was based on the premise of recognizing one's own ignorance. He famously stated, "I know that I am intelligent because I know that I know nothing."

This paradoxical wisdom—that awareness of our own ignorance is a form of intellectual humility—remains just as relevant today.

Admitting what you don't know ignites curiosity, fostering a hunger for knowledge that becomes the cornerstone of lifelong learning. It frees us from the self-imposed pressure of having to know everything, creating a space where we can ask questions, seek answers, and remain open to new ideas and perspectives. This attitude does more than just expand our knowledge; it nurtures resilience, adaptability, and a problem-solving mindset—all key attributes in today's rapidly evolving world.

Furthermore, acknowledging our ignorance is not just about our own learning—it also contributes to a healthier, more productive work environment. By publicly admitting our limitations, we model a culture of humility and continual learning. We create an environment where others feel safe to share their thoughts, contribute their ideas, and admit their own areas of ignorance.

Avoiding making others feel small when you're secure is not just an act of empathy—it's also a strategy for collective growth. Everyone benefits when knowledge is not a weapon but a shared resource. A culture that values humility over arrogance fosters a team that learns together, grows together, and consequently, succeeds together.

It's a simple yet powerful equation: humility plus ignorance equals growth. Admitting what we don't know provides the fuel for continuous learning. Meanwhile, our humility ensures that this process doesn't isolate others but instead fosters an environment of shared growth.

In the end, security does not come from pretending to know it all; it comes from acknowledging our ignorance and committing to learn. It comes from the understanding that our value is not diminished by what we don't know but is continually enhanced by our desire to learn and our humility to grow. In the journey of growth and learning, humility and ignorance are not just companions; they are guides, leading us toward endless possibilities and profound wisdom.

ᴁ Lesson 24

FIND YOUR STYLE

When I first began my career, I took a lot of heat for being too flashy. Serious hedge fund managers didn't like the fact that I was running around town, giving talks, and putting myself on television. They didn't like that I cursed too much, or that I enjoyed the spotlight.

Maybe they had a point.

But I didn't care then, and I don't care now.

For a great deal of my life—like, until my early twenties—I worried a lot about fitting in. When I wore the wrong kind of suit to a meeting and someone pulled me aside to tell me I looked like a jackass, I'd walk around with a crippling sense of shame for the next three days, minimum.

Then I realized something. If you dress like everyone else, you're going to be like everyone else. If you talk like everyone else, the chances that anyone's ever going to listen to you decline sharply. Don't get me wrong, though. Looking, talking, and acting like everyone else can be a good way to move up through the ranks at a company. In fact, when it comes to most office jobs, doing what everyone else is doing is probably your best bet, at least until you get the hang of your job and a sense of what you're supposed to be doing. I'm not telling you to get Post Malone–style face tattoos and walk into work every day with a parrot on your shoulder (or any live animals, for that matter).

But once you've learned the ropes at your job and learned them well, don't be afraid to bring a little of your personality to what you do. If you've got a big personality, as I've been told that I do (imagine that), then you're going to do things bigger than most people. The key here is knowing who you are and staying true to yourself. If you've got jokes that used to make your friends laugh, don't be afraid to break them out in the boardroom. If you're the kind of guy who likes to wear sweaters rather than suits, put on the sweaters and make yourself feel comfortable. Chances are, that'll make everyone else feel comfortable, too.

Over the course of my life, I've quoted the great F. Scott Fitzgerald quite often. Sometimes, I don't agree with him. I certainly don't agree with his assertion that "there are no second acts in American life," because I think there sure are. But most of the time, F. Scott knocks it out of the park, which he did when he said, "All Americans are self-invented."

It probably won't surprise you to learn that I think this is absolutely true.

Throughout this book, I've quoted a great deal from Marcus Aurelius's *Meditations.* That's because I don't think there's a better book in the world for people who want to learn to take on life in their own way, or to deal with the many challenges that a unique career—whether in business or the arts—can throw your way.

Late in that book, he addresses the issue of what to do when people don't quite get your vibe (although he doesn't say it exactly like that).

Nevertheless, Marcus Aurelius advises his reader—who, again, was really himself, given that the whole book is just a journal—to "get inside" the person who's giving you shit (although he didn't say it exactly like that). He reminds himself to "look at what sort of person [the guy who's giving you shit] is. You'll find you don't need to strain to impress him."

In other words, don't change because you think you need to fit in with what other people think of you. You're not going to please people who don't want you to succeed.

All you can do is succeed, and *then* see what they think of you.

And most importantly, succeed your way. Not anyone else's.

BE PRESENT

A few years ago, scrolling through Twitter, I heard about a new book called *Stolen Focus*, written by the journalist Johann Hari. Although I wasn't quite familiar with the work Hari had done in the past, which includes a memoir about addiction called *Chasing the Scream* that I've heard is excellent, the premise of his new book sounded intriguing.

According to a review in the *Washington Post*, the premise of *Stolen Focus* was as follows:

> We are collectively losing our capacity for sustained concentration...and the problem is getting worse every day. We're not present in our daily lives; not much gains traction in our minds. And we're not simply losing our focus: It's actively being stolen.

Yikes.

Reading those words, I felt a flash of recognition. For most of my life, I've considered myself to be someone whose ability to focus on complex tasks—not to mention long books and convoluted reports—was, at the very least, above average. But lately, I had noticed that my ability to keep my ass in a chair and look at one thing for any extended period of time was declining, and it was declining *fast.*

For a while, I chalked it up to old age. I figured that my brain was breaking down slowly in the same way my body was. It seemed to make sense that I could no longer make my way through a three-hundred-page book in two sittings the same way I could no longer bench press 225 pounds for reps or run a five-minute-mile.[ii] But I also had a nagging suspicion that my declining focus had something—and maybe everything—to do with the little glass square that I kept in my pocket at all hours of the day.

When I first got the iPhone, I thought it was a miracle of modern technology, which it is. Having subsisted on Blackberries for years, I found the user experience on Apple much more intuitive, and so I used it more. No longer did I have to sit quietly and wait for my subway car to pull into the next station. No longer was I forced to wait until I got to the office in the morning to start reading the financial news stories of the day. Everything I could ever want to know was right there in my pocket.

Then I downloaded Twitter onto the phone. Then Instagram. Then I started getting alerts from a bunch of apps that I didn't even know I downloaded. As my follower counts on social media platforms started to balloon, so did the time I was spending taking the phone out of my pocket to check in on how everyone was doing. Although I rarely spoke to my followers directly, there was a sense that I needed to be always in conversation with them. When something big happened in the world, I started to feel an urge to post—to contribute to the conversation. There was this weird sensation that if I didn't, I might disappear.

---

ii   Small Edit After Reviewing Lesson 11: I have never run a five-minute mile.

As it turns out, this isn't at all uncommon, especially when it comes to people who live in the public eye. Today, we're able to get real-time feedback about everything we say from millions of people, and we can talk right back to those millions of people when they say things we don't like. This is not something that human beings were ever meant to do, and it's killing us slowly.

If you've ever studied psychology, you might have heard of something called Dunbar's number, which was coined by an evolutionary psychologist at Oxford University named Robin Dunbar in the late twentieth century. According to a recent interview Dunbar did with *The Atlantic*, the number represents "the number of meaningful and stable relationships you can have at any one time. That includes extended family as well as friends....The number 150 is an average, but there's a lot of variation. The range of variation is somewhere between 100 and 250."

In other words, you're not supposed to have a million friends. In fact, you *can't* have a million friends. Even if you consider yourself the best networker in the world, the quality of your relationships will begin to degrade after you make your 251st friend. Of course, there are wrinkles to this. As Dunbar explains, you can have up to 1,500 acquaintances and still have healthy "relationships" with all of them, and you can recognize up to about 5,000 faces in the same way.

But the people you're going to have meaningful connections with? They're walking around your house right now. They're the ones whose names come up first when you open the Messages app on your phone. These are the people you should be prioritizing.

And yet we—meaning *I*—have spent way too much time focused on what strangers think about us. We've spent years living as if we're constantly performing for an audience, which, in a sense, we have been. Not only is that unhealthy for the relationships we're supposed to be prioritizing, it's also bad for our brains. If we're constantly thinking about the hundreds of thousands of people out on the internet and what they think about us, we're not going to be able to focus on the words in front of our faces.

This is especially true when it comes to reading anything of substance, which requires a certain degree of imagination and grit. Even the best books in the world can take a while to get into. I don't think there's anyone alive who can open up *War and Peace*, read the first few lines—which are written, oddly enough, mostly in untranslated French—and be absorbed in the world Tolstoy created right off the bat. These days, it takes a few pages, or a few hours, to sink into an old book and hear what the person who wrote it is trying to say.

If you're anything like me, that's been getting harder and harder in recent years.

So, when I saw that blurb for the book *Stolen Focus*, I immediately knew that I needed to read it. I wanted to know exactly how my attention was being "stolen," as the author claimed, and I wanted to get it back. I went straight to Amazon and started reading the blurb for the book, which says:

> In the United States, teenagers can focus on one task for only sixty-five seconds at a time, and office workers average only three minutes. Like so many of us, Johann Hari was finding that constantly switching from device to device and tab to tab was a diminishing and depressing way to live. He tried all sorts of self-help solutions—even abandoning his phone for three months—but nothing seemed to work. So Hari went on an epic journey across the

world to interview the leading experts on human attention—and he discovered that everything we think we know about this crisis is wrong.

We think our inability to focus is a personal fail-ure to exert enough willpower over our devices. The truth is even more disturbing: our focus has been stolen by powerful external forces that have left us uniquely vulnerable to corporations deter-mined to raid our attention for profit. Hari found that there are twelve deep causes of this crisis, from the decline of mind-wandering to rising pollution, all of which have…

And that's as far as I got.

Right around that sentence, my phone rang. Or maybe I got a Twitter notification. Whatever the distraction was, it came quickly, and it pulled me right out of the moment. I didn't even get the chance to buy the book.

So, unfortunately, I can't tell you what techniques Hari rec-ommends for getting your focus back. I can't take you through the twelve steps that he apparently lays out over the course of the book, which (based on the quick Google search I performed just now) got some pretty good reviews. Maybe you can go out and read it. Be sure to let me know what it says when you do.

Now, I could have skimmed the reviews of this book and pre-tended that I read it. I could have hired a researcher to comb through the book, pick out the good points, and send me a report; then I could have copied and pasted that report right into this book. You wouldn't have known the difference.

But I think it's important, as we near the end of this book of advice from me, that you understand just how much I struggle every day with the same things that everyone does. There are days when I fail to heed just about every lesson in this book. Sometimes I lie about little things because it's easy. Sometimes I don't attack my work with the kind of discipline that I'm suggesting you use to go after whatever it is that you want in life.

But every day, I get up and try again.

Do I sometimes get up a little later than I should? Sure. Do I still have trouble focusing on my work, my kids, and my fitness? Absolutely.

At this moment, I don't think that there's anything more difficult for people than staying in the moment. Given how many apps, YouTube videos, and hyper-realistic video games there are in the world, I don't know how anyone—especially anyone under the age of about eighteen or so—can develop the skills necessary to read a long article, have a complex argument, or think critically about a dense, complicated issue. Maybe that's why the tenor of our national arguments, political and otherwise, seems to have devolved over the past few years.

In part, this is because technology is designed to be addictive. This is especially true for social media. I don't think it'll be shocking to anyone to learn that when the engineers at Twitter and Facebook get together to plan a new piece of technology, they've got the weak spots of the human brain in mind. They design the user interfaces of these websites to work on the human brain in the same way that slot machines do. You "pull the lever," wait a few seconds, and immediately get some kind of reward—be it a like, a comment, or a post that shows you something interesting. Even if you don't see something you like, your brain always assumes that something you *do* like is just a few inches away. All you need to do is flick your thumb upward and wait.

According to a recent article for the University of Michigan's Institute for Healthcare Policy, a professor named Daniel Kruger pointed out that these methods are "so effective they can activate similar mechanisms as cocaine in the brain, create psychological cravings and even evoke 'phantom calls and notifications' where users sense the buzz of a smartphone, even when it isn't really there."

So, don't feel too bad about how addicted you are to your devices. They're designed to trap you in that way. But that doesn't mean that you're not still responsible for how much time you waste staring at your phone. As we discussed a few pages ago, just because companies "ought" not to design technology that rewires your brain in a bad way, making you crave more and more time with your phone with every swipe, that doesn't mean they're going to stop doing it.

Quite the opposite, in fact.

So, what do you do? How are you going to stop yourself from spending five or six hours out of every seventeen hours you're actually awake wasting time staring at a screen? How are you going to get back thirty percent of your productive time and learn to do something with it?

These are questions I ask myself every day.

Before we start thinking through strategies, let's look at how far we've come together.

First off, you're reading a book, which is a good start. And if you've arrived at this sentence after reading straight through from the very first page, (and you've been reading at a slow, deliberate pace, as suggested in Lesson 6), you've probably been staring at words on a page for just under eight hours now.

Great work.

Now, let's take a moment and think about how amazing that is. With all the distractions that are available to you—television, Twitter, and especially the ultra-addictive apps like TikTok and Instagram—you decided to spend the amount of time it takes to watch an entire season of a prestige HBO drama sitting and reading words that I crafted over a period of several months. You took the advice of great men such as Aurelius and Aristotle, who both believed that knowing yourself is the beginning of wisdom. And of course, there is Socrates, who once said that it is the wisest among us who admit they know nothing.

Now look up.

Wherever you are, look around the room (or the subway car, or the airplane cabin), and *really* think about what you see. Do it for a few minutes, and then come back.

I'll still be here.

If I'm right about this—and I sincerely hope that I am—the world probably looked slightly different than it did before you started your reading session. It certainly looked different than it might have if you'd spent the last few hours scrolling through your Instagram feed, looking for a quick dopamine hit. I'm willing to bet that you feel different, too. Even if you didn't like the book you just read, which I hope isn't the case, you do have a sense of accomplishment for having sat down and absorbed what I had to say.

And by the way, if you *did* hate it, that's still useful. Now, when you're faced with a tough situation, you can think back to the advice I've set out in these pages, laugh at how stupid I am, and try to do the opposite. See where that gets you.

Either way, you managed to sit and stay present, in the moment, long enough to absorb a book, which is much more than I can say for most people these days.

A while back, the online magazine *Slate* released some grim internal data showing how many of the people who started reading their articles finished them. According to the study, only 11 percent of the people who clicked on a long piece of writing managed to make it all the way to the end. In the years since, the tools that companies have for checking just how many people read—or watch—the content they put out have only gotten more advanced. As of this writing, in May of 2023, Netflix can not only tell whether you finished the latest season of *Stranger Things*, but they can also tell when you paused, when you fast-forwarded, and at what precise second you decided to shut the television off and go do something else.

Luckily, I don't have that kind of data. I'll never know how many people picked up this book, read a few pages, and decided I was pretty much just saying the same thing over and over again before they put it back on the shelf and gave up. That's probably a good thing.

So, congrats on making it this far with me. I hope you learned something along the way. Strange as it might sound, I did, too.

Primarily, I learned (again) that the most important thing in life is joy, and the pursuit of meaning. I also learned (again) that the only way to truly get these things is to wake up every day, give thanks for the things that you have, and acknowledge the fact that the sun came up this morning. For some people, it doesn't.

As for the struggle to be present, I don't have a lot of answers for you. As I said before, it's one of the things I still struggle with to this day. I've found over the past few years that meditation helps. So does leaving your phone at home every once in a while to go for a walk. If you have kids, bring them. If not, go meet someone, fall in love, and have some.

Or don't. It's really up to you.

If you're out there trying to figure out how to do your best in each moment—and you're not lying or cheating people—I think you'll get along just fine.

Good luck.

Appendix A

QUICK REFERENCE GUIDE

Look, I know that not everyone has the time—or the desire—to sit down and read almost three hundred pages straight through. Some people don't even have time to flip around this book aimlessly in search of a sentence or two that might apply to them.

You're busy. I get that.

So, if you've ended up at the back of this book looking for advice on a situation you're currently dealing with, or you're trying to solve a big problem and you don't know how, see if any of the following apply to you.

Have you just been...

Fired?

Don't worry. It happens to the best of us.

Meaning me.

I've been fired several times in my life, and I've always come back stronger than ever. If you want to hear about some of those times, check on Lessons 2 and 16.

Dumped?

Yikes. Sorry about that.

But you're going to be fine.

Flip right to Lessons 4, 5, 6, 21, and 22. Read them, and you'll be back in the game in no time.

Publicly shamed?

Boy, have you come to the right place.

First of all, you're going to be fine. Although the wrath of Twitter, cable news, and newspaper op-ed pages can feel pretty brutal while it's happening to you—especially if you pay attention to those things, which you shouldn't—I promise, it'll pass.

Turn your phone off, go for a walk, and wait out the storm. Try not to act too quickly.

And read Lessons 1, 3, 4, 5, and 6.

Made to feel stupid?

Keep your chin up and read Lesson 23.

Punched in the face?

Before you do anything, put some ice on it. Then go to Lesson 21.

Promoted?

Congrats! As you move forward in your new role, you'll need some skills. You can find them in Lessons 1, 2, 3, 4, 8, 9, and 11.

Appendix B

A READING LIST

You probably noticed that the pages of this book were stuffed—some might say *over*stuffed—with references to books. Sorry about that. Since I started up my podcast *Open Book*, I've had a hard time talking about anything else.

If you've enjoyed this book and you're wondering which ones to read next, or you want to go a little deeper on some of the concepts we've discussed so far, try this list. All the books on it are either (a) my favorite books of all time or (b) ones that I've enjoyed recently. Some of them were mentioned in the preceding pages; some weren't. Some are well-researched works of history, while some are pulse-pounding thrillers.

If there's a star next to the title, you can find an episode of my podcast in which the author and I have spoken at length about the content of the book.

Happy reading.

The 48 Laws of Power
By Robert Greene

As I said during my interview with Robert Greene, which I conducted in December of 2022, this is one of the most important books you can read if you're dealing with other people. At the simplest level, the book—which is really forty-eight small books in one—walks you through all the pitfalls of dealing with other people. You'll read thrilling stories about the tyrants of history who've attained power, misused it, and lost it. You'll also get some great advice on how to spot people who are looking to screw you over, which is always good.

The Power Broker
By Robert Caro

This book, which tells the full life story of the urban planner Robert Moses, will make you see New York City in a completely different light. If nothing else, you'll learn that almost every structure you see in that city—as well as most of the highways on Long Island—are the work of one strange, incredibly driven man.

Above anything else, the book is a masterful demonstration of how power works in American life.

The Rise of Theodore Roosevelt
By Edmund Morris

The first book in an excellent three-volume biography of the great Teddy Roosevelt, this book is still unmatched (in my opinion) when it comes to books about TR and what made him so great. Much of the Teddy Roosevelt section in Lesson 8--which tells the story of how Roosevelt built his body from a young age— is adapted from Morris's book. If you're looking to find out more about one of our greatest presidents, this is the place to start.

And Then There Was Light
By Jon Meacham

Deciding which book about Lincoln to include here wasn't easy. As you probably know, there are more biographies of Abraham Lincoln than there are on just about any other human being in American history.

There's good reason for that.

Perhaps more than anyone else, Abraham Lincoln epitomizes what is great about America. He educated himself using only used books, built his own law practice from nothing, and held the Union together at a time when it didn't seem at all likely he would succeed.

This book, by the great historian Jon Meacham—who's also written very well on President George H.W. Bush, among other key historical figures—tells the story of how Lincoln held the country together, stuck to his guns, and defied his critics.

The Rise and Fall of the Third Reich
By William Shirer

This is a massive book, both in terms of importance and actual size. (My paperback version runs just over one thousand pages.)

The book includes a complete, step-by-step account of how the Nazis seized power and how they eventually fell. Given that the author William Shirer was a correspondent in Germany at the time of Hitler's rise, many of his observations are recounted in the first person. Read it if you want to be chilled to the bone by how easy it was for an authoritarian regime to take power.

Just don't read it on the subway—the big swastika on the cover might send the wrong message to your fellow passengers—and definitely don't drop it on your foot.

The Age of Eisenhower
By William Hitchcock

Sadly, I didn't get to write very much about Dwight D. Eisenhower in this book. But I should have. The man is the best example of how to lead a disciplined, purposeful life as you're likely to find in recent memory, and this book does a phenomenal job of telling the story of that life.

Extraordinary Popular Delusions and the Madness of Crowds
By Charles Mackay

A book that everyone who's ever worked on Wall Street has probably read. Whether you want to work on Wall Street or not, I'd recommend reading it.

Meditations
By Marcus Aurelius

I mean, how many times did I quote this book in the pages you just read? Twenty? Thirty?

There's a reason for that.

So, go out and buy a copy of this book. Unlike most of what I've recommended here, it's not a long book and you can read it in small chunks. But it's so good, you probably won't want to.

The Madness of Crowds
By Douglas Murray

A deep, eloquent exploration of the strange, new social movements that had taken root on the American left. The author, who took his title from Charles Mackay's classic book, does a great job of getting to the root of what is driving people so crazy.

***Better Angels of Our Nature**: Why Violence Has Declined*
By Steven Pinker

Believe it or not, things are better than ever. There's never been a better time to be alive. Read this book by Steven Pinker and find out why.

Confidence Man
By Maggie Haberman

A book on Donald Trump by the woman who knows him better than anyone. For a long time, Maggie Haberman was the go-to reporter for all things Trump. In this book, she traces his life and explains how he got to be the way that he is.

Stolen Focus
By Johann Hari

Still haven't read this one.
If you do, let me know how it turns out.

Talking to Strangers
By Malcolm Gladwell

A great book by one of the top nonfiction writers of all time on why we fail so often when meeting new people, and how we can do better.

Those Angry Days
By Lynne Olson

Donald Trump was not the beginning. In this book, which chronicles the rise of Charles Lindbergh, the writer Lynne Olson tells us about the initial *America First* movement, and sheds light on where the second one is going in the process.

King: A Life
By Jonathan Eig

A great biography of one of the most admirable (and surprisingly complicated) men who ever lived: Martin Luther King, Jr. In this book, which is the product of many months of careful research, Jonathan Eig reconstructs the life of MLK, and gives us new perspective on why the man matters so much today.

Unshakable
By Tony Robbins

In terms of inspiring people to live up to their full potential, there's no one better than the great Tony Robbins. This guy is the GOAT, and this, in my opinion, is the finest book he's ever written.

*A Sacred Oath
By Mark Esper

Mark Esper is a kind, decent man who had the good sense to leave the White House on his own. This book gives an insight into his philosophy and includes some great stories about his career.

*City of Fire
By Don Winslow

As discussed, Don Winslow is one of the greats when it comes to crime writing. In this thriller, he elevates the genre he perfected over so many decades in the business and begins a trilogy that will endure for years to come.

Undermoney
By Jay Newman

One of the finest thrillers ever written about the world of high finance.

Anna Karenina
By Leo Tolstoy

Asked near the end of his life what the greatest novel ever written was, the Russian writer Vladimir Nabokov said, "Anna Karenina, Anna Karenina, Anna Karenina." I think he was right. This book, which contains far more humanity (and fewer pages) than Tolstoy's other great work *War and Peace*, is one of the most rewarding I've ever read.

The Sportswriter
By Richard Ford

On the surface, this novel is about a sportswriter who doesn't love his job and wants more from life. Beneath the surface, it's a meditation on life, love, and loss that you'll never forget.

The Great Gatsby
By F. Scott Fitzgerald

One of my personal favorites, which just so happens to take place in my backyard.

ACKNOWLEDGMENTS

This book could not have happened without my erstwhile editor Debra Englander. For the past fourteen years, she has put up with me and edited, and in some cases redrafted, parts of my books. I am very grateful to her and her team at Post Hill. Sean McGowan found my voice and was the principal architect of this book, so many thanks for his help as well. Additionally, my agent, Ian Kleinert, who always finds a publisher willing to produce my writings.

Lastly to my family. Let's face it, I can be a workaholic, sometimes insular and aloof as I am trying to juggle too many things at once. My high school math teacher, Mr. Weickel, once wrote in my yearbook that I would "try to put a gallon of water in a one quart bottle." It not only says what his opinion was of my capacity but he was spot-on related to my lifelong habits. Being loved unconditionally by my broo; it is the greatest gift in my life. I just want them to know that I reciprocate in that love every minute of every day.